Live a Life of No Regrets

Suzie Hayman

Also available in ebook

With thanks to the brave and sometimes heartbreakingly honest contributors who told me about their regrets through an anonymous questionnaire and face to face. And as ever to my husband Vic, about whom I have no regrets.

Live a Life of No Regrets

Suzie Hayman

Before becoming a freelance journalist, Suzie Hayman trained as a teacher and worked for the Family Planning Association and then Brook Advisory Centres as Press and Information Officer. Her first column as an agony aunt was with *Essentials* magazine, before she moved on to *Woman's Own*. She has been a columnist for BBC Health Online, the Saturday *Guardian* and *The Times*, and is now am agony aunt for *Woman Magazine*. She trained as a counsellor with Relate, and as an accredited parenting educator with Triple P (Positive Parenting Programme). She is a spokesperson and trustee for the major UK parenting charity Family Lives, and a trustee of The Who Cares? Trust, for 'looked after' children.

Suzie makes frequent appearances on national and local television and radio, as a counsellor and agony aunt.

Contents

Introduction   xi

1 Regrets   1
What do we regret?
Feelings of failure
Your early years – how regrets can start
Resilience
Lost opportunities
The need for resilience
Lack of resilience
Teaching resilience
What you can and can't change
Past experiences
Following in the pattern
Life/work balance
Why time is so important
Top tips to help you achieve a life/work balance
What are your regrets about?

2 'I wish I had made enough time for my family'   23
Memories of the past
What's missing?
Family time
Making things work for you
Social media
Your Action Plan: Step 1 – identify your main regrets
Top tips for being regret free

3 'I wish I had kept in touch with my friends'   45
The support network
Finding and building a support network
Online friendships
Recurrent problems in friendships and how to deal with them
Top tips for making and keeping friends
Your Action Plan: Step 2 – say sorry

4 'I wish I had pursued my dreams and ambitions'   73
'When I grow up...'
Settling for second best
Is it too late to change?
Fulfilling your dreams and inspiring others

Your Action Plan: Step 3 – confront and accept what has
led to your regrets
Top tips to help you make up for lost time

5 'I wish I'd spoken up'   87
Communication – or the lack of it!
Don't make assumptions
Not expressing our feelings
Communication skills and taking risks
Standing up for yourself
Do you communicate?
Top tips for improving your communication skills
Your Action Plan: Step 4 – consider your relationships
'Toxic' relationships

6 'I wish I'd managed my money better'   109
Being poor
Money's place in our society
Money as a means of control or manipulation
The emotional 'weight' of money
Putting money in its proper place
Money and the young
Money and the nearly-adult
Money and regrets
How to make and balance a budget
Your Action Plan: Step 5 – grieve for your regrets
Top tips

**7 'I wish I'd thought about my
relationships better'**   129
Intimate relations
The importance of self-confidence
We all need approval
Trust yourself
Divorce or counselling?
Ten top tips for making your relationship work
Over-praising our children
The value of descriptive praise
Top tips for improving relationships
Your Action Plan: Step 6 – learn from your regrets

8 'I wish I had made my body a temple!' 149
Healthy living
Eating well
Move it!
Drinking...
...and smoking
What's important?
Body art
Body changes
Your Action Plan: Step 7 – cherish yourself

9 'So what can I do about it?' 169
Taking action
What can you do? – Revisit your Action Plan
If you could go back, what advice would you have for
  your younger self?
Final word

Appendix: A list of organizations that
can provide help 191
Index 203

Introduction

'Never regret. If it's good, it's wonderful. If it's bad, it's experience.'

Victoria Holt (who wrote as, among other names, Jean Plaidy and Phillipa Carr)

Most of us have regrets in our lives. Our sorrow over chances missed or opportunities fudged can be essentially fleeting – 'That cupcake looked so lovely – why did I say no?' – or the spur to future action – 'I wish I'd thrown caution to the winds and gone surfing last holiday!' More often, they can be about issues where we've missed the boat entirely and for good: 'I wish I'd said yes to that boy who asked me out when I was 16' or 'I never should have thrown that dress away!' Sometimes, our regrets can be more serious: 'If only I'd not got into the car with my drunken friend' or 'I should have reconciled with my mother before she died.'

Listening, as I do as an agony aunt and counsellor, to people who look back, not in anger but with sadness, it's easy to see some themes emerge again and again, and how the older you get the more reproachful and even the angrier you can be about opportunities lost. Do we mourn the chance to have driven that fast car or worn that amazing outfit while we still could? Or regret not spending enough time with our children, or letting our dreams and aspirations go, or being unable to express our feelings to those we love? One American friend said to me: 'I regret that I didn't choose a theatrical academy instead of university. I regret not accepting a free trip to England, Italy and France. False pride about being able to pay one's own way got the better of me. And – oh yes, I regret giving back that sapphire-and-gold ring at break-up!'

Regrets can spoil your life in two ways. It can be because of the sense of loss or resentment or anguish over the source of regret itself – the pain at losing touch with or hurting someone you loved, of missing out on something, of making a wrong choice. But regrets can also hurt you simply by becoming themes or obsessions in your life – it's not the lost chance or missed opportunity, the wrong word or bitter disappointment that is the problem, but the very fact that it is as if you spend your whole life stuck, looking backwards and unable to move on. Regrets can trip you up in so many ways. Sometimes you're caught going over and over the 'what might have beens' and the 'if onlys'. Like Lot's wife, transformed into a pillar of salt as she turned back to look at her lost home, it's the act of looking back that spoils what you have in the present. Often, a habit of risk aversion and cowardliness not only puts you in a regretful situation now, it prevents you doing any better in the future.

Looking at what we regret, why and how, is not just about examining the past; it's about doing better from now onwards. Regrets and disappointment so often manifest themselves as anger and resentment, and can lead to a relationship and parenting style that tends towards confrontation, which hurts you and hurts those around you.

That's why I decided to write this book. Again and again, I have seen people mired in depression and resentment, musing on episodes in their life that they regret and unable to look forward to the rest of their lives with much optimism. So many times we make the wrong priorities and the wrong choices. Maybe it's because we feel that we must get on with the business of earning a living and getting by, and that somehow certain aspects of our lives can be put on the back burner and dealt with later. All too often, by the time we want to focus on those aspects, it's too late. Couples feel their own relationship has to take second place to bringing up their families, and that they'll pick it up again when the children leave home. More times than not, they discover that they've lost contact with each other and that there's no relationship to return to, when the time finally comes. Individuals feel they have to bypass keeping up friendships because life is so busy, and when they retire and want to share a coffee, play some golf, go to the cinema, there's nobody to do it with because they've lost touch. And so many people opt for the safe route, letting ambition and aspiration take a back seat, and then wish they had taken risks or simply tried it out. Nobody ever said on their deathbed, 'I wish I'd spent more time cleaning the house…' but plenty say, 'I wish I'd spent more time with my family, my partner, my friends…'

As well as using quotes from letters and interviews over many years of experience in helping people redress problematical situations, I asked a range of people to answer some questions on their regrets, in confidence, on the Internet site SurveyMonkey. I don't pretend this is in any way an exhaustive or representative piece of research – the sample was self-selected from people who saw my appeal on Facebook and Twitter, or had the link sent on to them by people who had done so or with whom I had some connection. It was, however, interesting in that it both confirmed much of what we already know about regrets, and added some ideas and suggestions that were new to me. Above all, it gave me some authentic voices to add to mine in saying that we need to look at our regrets, in order, perhaps, to stop them controlling us.

So this book is about reducing your regrets. It's about looking at what you might regret now or in the future and helping you make changes now to address that disappointment, that sense of loss, that present and future dissatisfaction. I'll look at why we have regrets, what are the main regrets and what we might do to make sure that we don't come to the end of our lives looking back in sadness. We all have regrets – this is about making sure it's only the small stuff we wish had been different, while avoiding or redressing the significant life regrets that can leave us feeling emotionally crippled, or having really missed out on some of life's chances.

The question I will be asking will be 'Are you happy?' If the answer is yes, then clearly you should keep on doing whatever it is you're doing! But if the answer is no, or 'Yes, but I wish I had…', then maybe this book is for you, because you need to change something. The issue is: do we accept that everyone has disappointments and doubts and that these are a part of life, or do we fight back? My aim will be to help you, the reader, and through you those you love, to craft an **Action Plan**. No matter what stage of life you are in, there will be ways in which you can take control so that you are left feeling less disappointed. Clearly, the earlier you act to banish the opportunity for regrets to have a chance to grow the better, but that's not to say it's ever too late – making better choices even at the eleventh hour can make significant differences to us, our families and those around us. There's no point looking back simply to bemoan our fate, but there's every point in using our pasts to inform our actions now and in the future, and in offering insight and encouragement to our own children so that they don't make the same mistakes.

> *Grant me the serenity to accept the things I cannot change,*
> *The courage to change the things I can,*
> *And wisdom to know the difference.*

Some things you cannot go back and make any different. Some things you can change by altering the way you look at them or the hold they have over you. And some things you most certainly can alter, significantly and profoundly. The trick is to work out which is which, and how to swing the balance. That is what we will be exploring in these pages.

The Teach Yourself Breakthrough series has a number of features to help you get the most out of reading this book. *Live a Life of No Regrets* includes the following boxed features:

 'Key idea' boxes that distil the most important ideas and thoughts

 'Remember this' boxes to help you take away what really matters

 'Try it now' boxes to provide you with useful exercises and techniques

 'Case study' boxes to give you real-life examples of how people dealt with an issue

 'Self-assessment' boxes with quiz questions with which to assess yourself

 'Focus points' at the end of each chapter to help you hone in on the core message of each chapter.

At the end of the book you will also find an appendix that lists organizations providing further information and help.

1

Regrets

In this chapter you will learn:

▶ *The nature of regrets and what to do about them*

▶ *How a lifestyle can make regrets start to grow*

▶ *How your early years and your family can be the starting point of regrets*

▶ *How to develop the resilience needed to minimize regrets in the future.*

What do we regret?

Most of us have regrets, of some sort and of varying degrees. One respondent to my questionnaire said 'Je ne regrette rien', somewhat defiantly, and it's clearly true that some people do go through life serenely unaffected by the turns of fortune that have happened to them or the mistakes they might have made. Whether it's from confidence, fatalism or because they've taken to heart that old joke that, if you're not panicking, it's because you don't know what's going on, they seem to be able to manage the negative emotions about their past that many of us find hard to control.

Other respondents recognized that dwelling on regrets can be a futile pastime – they simply form part of the background that got you where you are now. As one respondent said: 'I have regrets, but since I've ended up with my ideal partner (and I say that after 37 years of being together!) I couldn't and wouldn't change anything. If things had been different and I'd had a less awful time of it while growing up, I'd never had gone down the route that brought me to him.'

But the reality is that many of us do look back and wish some aspects of our life were different. It's not just about what might have happened many years ago, but how those events or behaviour patterns continue to play a part in your life now, and will do in the future. Frequently, if you don't consider and recognize where things might have gone wrong, you can't put certain issues right for the present and the future.

Regrets can be about sins of commission or omission – things done or not done. One person said to me, 'I never beat myself up over things I haven't done', while several agreed that 'My regrets fall into both camps but I'd say the most significant are things I've done.' But, for most, it was the chances missed, the opportunities passed by, that left lingering sadness.

> 'Twenty years from now you will be more disappointed by the things you didn't do than by the ones you did do. So, throw off the bow lines. Sail away from the safe harbour. Catch the trade winds. Explore. Dream. Discover.'
>
> Mark Twain

Feelings of failure

What do most people feel that they have failed to do? Many people I discussed this with could pinpoint issues they wished they'd done differently: 'Being too afraid to take chances when they were offered to me', 'Not having travelled more', 'Not studying harder at school', 'Arguing with my mum quite so much', 'I wish I'd returned that phone call!' Lack of confidence, lethargy and passivity, fear of embarrassment and paying more attention to what you feel other people will think than what you really want come up again and again. We tend to look back and mourn the boy- or girlfriends we might have had, the fun times we could have shared and the experiences spoiled or which we denied ourselves. But, more than that, so many people see these losses as the beginning of a trend or a habit, that take us away from being able to step forward, speak up for ourselves and make the choices that would be best for us – not just then but now and in the future.

What is interesting is that many of us struggle to differentiate between the things we could have had power over and those we could not control. This also applies to the things we might now be able to address and those we cannot. Sometimes, there is nothing you could have done, and nothing you can do now. Sometimes, however, you need to get creative, perhaps to change the effect of one of those issues that you had no control over happening, or to stop it at least having a hold on you now.

Remember this: You can't change the past

We often regret things we couldn't have changed, but while it's perfectly valid to wish things had been different, there is no point in blaming or beating ourselves up about what happened. Save your energy for doing something about the here and now or the future – you can't change the past.

Your early years – how regrets can start

There can be no doubt that the family you are born into, the parenting you receive, the quality of the support, attention and love you are given and, indeed, the resources available to you can have a significant effect on your start in life. Living in poverty or living with parents who struggle to acknowledge and respond to your needs can have a significant effect on your life chances.

Case study: Serena

Serena can never remember even one time her mother ever hugged or kissed her, or praised or thanked her. She and her sister, two years older than her, fought for their mother's attention and both were convinced the other was the favourite. When they finally became friends and allies in their thirties they realized that neither had received much in the way of nurturing or consideration from their mother when young. Their father left when they were six and eight, but both Serena and her sister feel that, even before their mother had to struggle as a single parent, they were resented and looked on as a burden and an encumbrance. After their father had gone, they had the distinct impression she blamed them. Both have grown up as 'compulsive rescuers' – people who in their home and work life feel it's their responsibility to look after others, put their own needs last and make everything right. But they always feel guilty and that they are not doing enough.

At 42, on the brink of divorce, Serena finally gave in to her husband's insistence that they seek counselling. It was only then that she was able to look clearly at her lifelong regrets about her childhood, and the way they affected how she behaved in her relationship and with her family. Serena's regrets were that she had never been able to stop her father leaving, or bring him back into the family, and that her mother had not loved her as much as she would have liked. She worked tirelessly as a social worker, trying to keep families together. Her long hours, high levels of stress and perpetual feelings of failure meant she was often far too tired or distracted to give full attention to her husband and children, which then fuelled even more guilt and feelings of failure as her own family approached meltdown. It was only when she was challenged to consider what exactly she could have done in her own family, and how much her mother's lack of love was her mother's responsibility and lack of empathy rather than Serena's fault, that she could reassess her regrets. And that led to her reassessing her demands on herself.

The reality was that all her attempts at making it right for other families were really about wishing to go back and change her own childhood.

It was as though she felt that, if she could keep one family together, it might mean she had rewritten the script that ended with her own father leaving. But, of course, even if she'd had a perfect record in rescuing other people, it still wouldn't have changed her own past.

Once she saw that, Serena could begin to relax and forgive herself, and to stop having such unrealistic expectations of herself. She could also go and share her discoveries with her sister who was also trapped in the same situation. Both let go of the past and concentrated on the present and future, focusing on their own families, who became far happier, more demonstrative and loving, and more like the family she had always wished she had had.

Resilience

The family you happen to be born into can have profound effects on whether you develop resilience – the ability to cope with what life throws at you. Not having had the chance to develop resilience can mean that even small setbacks can be blown up out of all apparent proportion. One client of mine, Deirdre, remembered losing a stuffed toy at university:

> *I'd never had a teddy bear and having seen this one I'd asked for it and my boyfriend bought it for my birthday. Then, we were going to a friend's twenty-first and we suddenly realized we hadn't got her anything. He talked me into giving up my bear – he said he'd buy me a new one as soon as the weekend was over. Although I gave it away, because I had no choice, I was devastated. In fact, I never forgave him.*

Of course, it wasn't the bear so much as what it represented – the love and affection, comfort and security lacking in her childhood and now apparently not as present as she'd hoped in this relationship – that caused the real hurt.

It's not uncommon for people to say 'I regret being born into a poor family' or 'I wish my parents had been different.' One said:

> *When I look back, my pervading sense as a child was confusion and fear. I simply never understood what my parents wanted from me because, to be honest, it changed from day to day or minute to minute. It left me*

*with a lifelong suspicion and wariness towards friends
and partners. I was always waiting for them to move the
goalposts and start demanding impossible things. That's
what I was used to, after all.*

Another said:

*When I was in my late twenties I met a woman at work
who became a great friend, who was old enough to be
my mother. She had children of her own but we had this
wonderful relationship where she was part great friend, and
part mother substitute. I so envied her children – I wished
she had been my mother.*

Another acknowledged the fact that this was not something
over which you had any choice: 'My regret is over something
out of my control: how poor my family are and growing up in
a household that is overcrowded and devoid of any culture.'
So this does throw up an important issue – that, while you can
clearly have control over what you do now, and use a realization
of how your past experiences have affected your present
behaviour and beliefs to change, how much can you redress
what happened to you in your past? We shall consider that later.

Lost opportunities

Lost opportunities can continue to rankle years later:

*When I was 17 I had a deep email relationship with a boy
but was too afraid and embarrassed to take him up on the
offer to spend a week's holiday at his house. I made excuses
to avoid him and never told him how I felt about him. I
wish I had just embraced the opportunities I was given –
who knows, if I had gone to stay with him that week then I
might have had an amazing boyfriend back then. The thing
I regret is that we are no longer in touch and yet I hear
things about him occasionally and he sounds to be living a
really fascinating life and having lots of fun. I wish we were
still friends!*

Frequently, our regrets become set in stone from having been
mulled over, revisited and repeated. It's as if we create a script
and the longer we tell it to ourselves, the more fixed it becomes.

The relationship or experience you remember was, or would have been, one of unalloyed joy, the lost partner a paragon, and, if only you could go back or indeed get in touch, all would be well. And there may be some truth – after all, if this was a person or an opportunity you passed up because of shyness or anxiety it might have been one that could have brought you significant happiness. But, equally, it could have been simply one set of signposts on a road and you took another route, with similar signposts. You got to the same destination, just with different encounters along a different way. With the advent of the Internet and its possibilities for researching and getting back in touch with old acquaintances, many people have found to their cost that the person they've carried a torch for, for so long, turns out to be just as ordinary as the people they ended up with.

Key idea: Beware nostalgia

Sometimes going back to revisit a place or to rerun an experience ends in disaster as we find it wasn't as wonderful as we thought it should be or remembered it to be.

The need for resilience

One of the important aspects about whether regrets hold us back or not – as already touched on – is whether we have resilience. What do we mean by this? Resilience is the ability to recover from setbacks, the capacity to bounce back and carry on when things go wrong or you feel sad, put upon, out of step or out of sorts. It's also the ability to adjust – to be flexible and go with the flow, and not to worry or be upset when plans change or the situation deteriorates. Resilient people can cope when all around is falling to pieces and everything is awry. In contrast, if you have little resilience, you may find yourself going to pieces when the smallest and most trivial issue changes.

And what makes you resilient or not? Imagine building a tower of bricks. If you build one in a pyramid shape, with a wide and solid base tapering to a point, you can push and prod it, huff and puff at it all you want and it won't fall down. Remove a few bricks from the base and nothing happens. But what if you build your tower high and narrow, with just two or three bricks at the foundation? Blow on it, and it will likely come crashing down. Or slide a brick out from the bottom and the same thing happens. The key to the success or otherwise of both towers is the foundation. Something solid and interlocked will withstand pressure from outside and within. Something fragile and fragmentary is at risk. If you build the foundations of your life solidly, you will be resilient. Children who are loved and given attention and approval, who are helped to build self-esteem and self-confidence, will be resilient. Resilience comes, not from never having setbacks or failures or problems, but from having had the opportunity to encounter and overcome them while knowing you are approved of and supported.

Key idea: Experience and resilience

Being allowed to experience failure is one of the best ways to build resilience. When you are wrapped up in cotton wool and shielded from risk, or are never allowed to make mistakes, you never learn how to deal with them – how to do better, and how to accept the need to confront and challenge yourself and your abilities.

Children who are cosseted become over-anxious and scared of failure. Being overprotected tells you that you are right to feel overly frightened of a situation, a person, a thing. Instead of gaining the skills to tackle whatever are your fears, you make avoidance and blame your coping mechanisms.

Lack of resilience

Lack of resilience can come about when children are overprotected, or when they are given insufficient support to face the world. Children with parents who find it hard to be loving, who have problems of their own that means they do not pay as much attention to their children as they should, who are judgemental or critical or authoritarian, may all grow up with shaky foundations. They may be needy and self-critical, have low self-esteem and self-confidence, and be ready to crumble when put under pressure. And without resilience, even small pressures, or memories of issues from the past, can provoke unhappiness... and regrets. Of course, lack of resilience can also come about from having experienced traumatic events or losses. Long-term illness, serious accidents – for yourself or people important to you – or the loss of someone you love can all dent your confidence and bring about difficulties in dealing with even everyday issues, let alone tricky ones.

But resilience is a complex structure. Some people who have suffered the most appalling trauma or losses exhibit the ability to ride over it and not just survive but thrive. That's often because their background has given them the strong foundations to feel that, even when things go wrong, they can manage. However, even those who have come from unsupportive backgrounds sometimes show such resilience. It's a bit like swimming. Thrown in at the deep end, you'll be fine if you've been shown how to swim and given the confidence to know you can do it. You're at terrible risk of going under if you've never been taught. But sometimes simply thrashing around does the trick and you teach yourself. And, of course, you can always learn late in life. So, while having or not having developed resilience at an early age can explain why you might find yourself having regrets, and why some people can be seriously affected by regrets over issues others may think of as trivial, the good news is that you don't have to put up with the hand you have been dealt.

Key idea: Resilience and maturity

Whether you are able to bounce back and take things in your stride, or whether you will dwell on and let past regrets affect you later in life, often depends on the resilience you were or were not helped to build earlier in life. However, growing older might bring you confidence, experience and skills and help you build that ability afterwards.

Teaching resilience

How can you go about instilling resilience into your own children, and awakening it in yourself if you haven't gained it at an early age?

DON'T SAY 'EVERYTHING WILL BE ALL RIGHT'

False or all-embracing assurances won't persuade you or your children that things will work out. What can work is asking the questions that uncover an anxiety, and thinking through the fears. Ask open questions such as 'What worries you about this' / 'What worries you most about this?' Ask: 'Have you felt like this before? When and how did it turn out?' Simply confronting and analysing a fear often diminishes it. What this technique helps you do is get into the habit of thinking things through – first the problem, and then in testing and considering various solutions. Once you test the limits of a problem by looking at solutions, you acknowledge that it probably can be resolved. That in itself puts you in a far more powerful frame of mind.

Remember this: Open and closed questions

A **closed question** is one that can be answered with a yes, a no or a grunt. It can be apparently a genuine attempt to communicate, such as in 'Did you have a good day today?' Often, however, closed questions are in fact a statement rather than a query, such as 'What sort of a time do you call this?' and 'You don't think you're going out in that?' Whatever, the problem with closed questions is that they tend to shut down conversation rather than open it up.

In contrast, an **open question** gives space for a response such as 'Tell me about your day.' They're not just about facts and figures but feelings and opinions. An open question makes it clear that you're listening and care about what the other person is thinking and feeling. Unlike a closed question such as 'Did you have a good day?', the open question 'Tell me about your day' allows the other person to pick on the aspect they'd like to describe or discuss and will often bring up far more, and far more significant, issues than a closed question ever could.

TRUST IN THE ABILITY TO HAVE THE ANSWERS

Children often fail to develop resilience because they have never been trusted. It may cause you anxiety but it's really important to let children carry the full cup from sink to table – dashing in saying 'Let me do that, darling – you'll spill it!' not only never allows the child to build the ability to manage such things but convinces them that, on so many other levels, they can't do it as well as you, so why try? By 'respecting the struggle' and letting them try, we not only allow them to learn the practical, physical skills, we also build in them the emotional skills of trying, failing, recognizing that it's not so bad and trying again. The sensible thing for adults to do in such a situation is make sure that the cup is an unbreakable one, that the liquid is water so it won't stain, and that there's a cloth at hand. If you get into the habit of supporting your children to be in control and to make choices for themselves, helping them when they need it but basically respecting their abilities, we help them build resilience.

And we can bring this into our own lives, too. Trusting a child to carry a cup of water and trusting your spouse to be able to read the map are basically the same things. What it says is: 'I know you can do it – I know I'm not the only one with these abilities. I'll support you if you need some help, but you can do it, too.'

MAKE PROBLEM SOLVING A KEY SKILL

As the proverb goes, 'It's better to light a candle than curse the dark'. As Deirdre says:

> My therapist has taught me something that is now a family joke, which is 'Don't look for problems, look for solutions.' Now, whenever I start moaning about something going wrong, or when anyone in the family does, we chorus this and it works. We start looking for what we can do about it rather than wasting energy on complaining. It's amazing how often, and how quickly, you can solve a problem if you only look for the solution instead of going on about it.

Asking your children, and yourself, to sit down, examine a situation, break it down into accessible chunks and then work out what to do is what works.

THE MAGIC WAND

It can be hard to bounce back when we feel that everything is hopeless and that we're helpless. The reality is that sometimes there is no solution to a particular problem. In such a situation, say 'I wish I had a magic wand. If I did, I'd wave it and make this all right.' Being reassured that someone cares and would put it right if they could can, strangely enough, frequently make you feel better. It allows you to recognize that there is another way of resolving a situation – accepting that, while it cannot change, your assessment of it can. If it can't be altered, accept it and pass on.

WHAT'S THE WORST THAT CAN HAPPEN?

We can often feel so overwhelmed, not necessarily by the situation at hand but what we think it will lead to. A child can be obsessing over exams and already anticipating failing, losing out on further education and a job and a happy life, or losing your love and approval. You can be consumed by anxieties over a job promotion, and convinced that you won't get it and will lose your job and soon be destitute. Becoming resilient can teach you to cast a realistic eye over the worst-case scenario. What would happen if you failed in this? Would it necessarily lead on to other problems? How likely is it to happen? What can you do about it? The worst case is in fact feeling helpless. Asking yourself 'What if...?' puts you back in power and able to manage.

IT'S OK TO FAIL

In trying not to have people feel failures, we seem to have created a culture in which nobody is allowed to fail. In fact, being shielded from failure does not build self-confidence or self-esteem. On the contrary, children – and thus adults – become disinclined to try, thinking that if failure is such a destructive thing that we are protected from it, then we don't want to risk courting it. And, if we never fail, what's the point of trying? Failure is the best incentive to learn.

Make mistakes and we will remember the correct solution far better than if it had been given to us. Make a hash of something and then go on to do better and we learn how to perfect skills. Trip up and then go one better and we learn that persistence pays off, and that we can raise ourselves up by our own efforts. Fail and we learn that putting in effort and taking part is often far more important than the final achievement. We can't all be gold-medal winners, but we can still run the race and enjoy our personal bests. Resilience is built on failure, and this makes having the courage to fail one of your best attributes.

Case study: Paul and Dot and Jenny

Paul and Dot's daughter Jenny was at what all the parents in the area said was a marvellous primary school – supportive, encouraging and non-competitive. They moved house just before she went to secondary school and it was a shock to all the family to find her in a school with a much harder edge, where pupils did not all get gold stars at sports day and where she was given failing marks for the first time. She was distressed and fed up and Dot raised the issue at the first parents' evening. One of Jenny's teachers pointed out that Jenny was very prone to give up easily and had little resilience, and she put it down to her never having had the experience of needing to try hard since all her previous efforts had been praised and welcomed, no matter what. The teacher reassured Dot and Paul – and Jenny – that she would adjust to the new situation and, in the long run, thrive with it. By the following year her results had improved, but, more importantly, Jenny was gaining real self-confidence and self-esteem by having to make efforts to do well.

Remember this: Points to consider

▶ The more self-aware you are about what you really want and what you are doing, the more you will avoid regrets in your later life.

▶ Lack of resilience is the main cause of regrets – developing it is the best protection against them.

▶ The family you are born into can have a profound effect on whether you develop resilience or become prone to regrets.

▶ Early lost opportunities can rankle years later.

What you can and can't change

When you are looking at regrets, perhaps the most important start is to think about what you can change and what you can't. You can't alter the family you were born into. However much you may wish you could, and however much you might fret or grind your teeth about it, you can't change whether they were well off or poor, whether they gave you home-cooked meals or frozen meals, whether they introduced you to books and classical music or not, or whether they were loving and nurturing. Blaming people in your past for their failures and making regrets about the way these issues might have harmed or held you back a central theme of your life does nothing but harm you. You might at some point benefit from facing people from your past with your unhappiness at some of the ways they might have behaved to you – of that, more later – but some aspects may be beyond their power to have changed, in which case you are, as the saying goes, 'spitting in the wind' (and you know what happens when you do that, don't you?).

Past experiences

The reason unhappy experiences in our past so often affect us is twofold. One is that we blame ourselves. It's natural and normal for children to be self-centred and feel the universe revolves around them, begins and ends with them. This can be very sweet and charming but also very destructive when a child is badly treated. Having love withheld, being criticized, judged and always coming up short and having unrealistic expectations put on them results in children feeling that they are unlovable, incapable and incompetent. The child doesn't judge and criticize the person doing this – they judge and criticize themselves. Regrets so often revolve around lack of attention or missing out:

> 'I wish my mum had loved me – I've spent so many years wondering what I'd done wrong or differently from my brother, who she doted on. When she was ill towards the end she'd go on and on about when he was visiting, how marvellous he was. He never did a damn thing for her while I looked after her.'

> 'I wished I'd got to know my dad's parents before they passed away. They died when I was eight and I've always thought I should have gone to see them more. Which I know is silly – how can an eight-year-old make the choices to visit people a hundred miles away? My mum should have arranged it, but I still blame myself.'

Key idea: The perils of self-blame

So often, it's not the issue itself that harms us – the pain at having missed or lost out, the grief at disappointed expectations – but the fact that we feel we should have been able to do something about it. It's that sense of self-blame and failure that rankles and harms.

Key idea: Dealing with the past

You can't go back and alter the past. Dealing with this sense of resentment and self-reproach can, however, allow you to change the way you see it and interpret those issues, and make different choices for yourself and those around you for the future. We'll look at this in more detail in later chapters but, once you can accept you can't change certain events, you can alter the way you blame yourself or others for them, and shrug off the way they influence your feelings and behaviour.

Following in the pattern

The other reason unhappy experiences in our past so often affect us is that we follow suit. The very thing we mourn or wish had been different becomes the pattern that we live our lives by, and that we insist those around us follow. 'I've always regretted being someone who avoids risk.' says Laura.

> 'I've said no to a family skiing holiday because flying scares me, let alone getting on skis, and I know I've missed out and caused my family to miss out, too. And I wouldn't apply for a promotion because I was scared I wouldn't get it – my husband says I'm silly because so what if I was refused? I'd be no worse off and might be better. But I can't help it. And now I realize I'm passing on the exact same attitude to our children. Their father is in despair about the times they'll pass up invitations or refuse to try things out... and I know it's my fault; I've done that to them.'

Ben is another example:

> 'The one thing I regret more than being a smoker myself was the fact that my son copied me and took up smoking when

he was a teenager. He's now 45 and has children and has, at last, been smoke free for a year, but I know it took him 20 years to get rid. He used to complain when he was little about me smoking, but even that, and all the health education in the world, can't stack up against wanting to be like your dad.'

However much such behaviour may feel set in stone, rewriting the script and altering a pattern can, in fact, be done. Ben himself was able to show his son how to give up smoking by example, and both were relieved when his son did it before Ben's grandsons were old enough to be aware of their father smoking. How you can become conscious of, challenge and confront and eventually change patterns set early in life will be covered in later chapters.

Life/work balance

Even in a recession, one of the modern ills seems to be that we're 'money rich but time poor' – we might be better off than previous generations, but we have far less free time. One of the big regrets many people have is that they are constantly torn between the pressures of employment and the needs of their personal life. We have to earn a living, but we also want quality time for our partners, our family, our friends and ourselves. It can feel as though there just aren't enough hours in the day or days in the week. And while we rush around trying to fit more and more activities into less and less time, it is often our couple and family relationships that suffer. So often this leads to bitter regrets later in life. We may have felt that keeping our relationships alive and healthy was something we could put on the back-burner. As one person said to me:

'I kept telling myself I could come back to my wife and children when I'd got my work life sorted to – that my priority surely was in making a success of that. When I finally had time it was too late – my wife said she no longer knew me or even wanted to make the effort, and my kids looked on me as a stranger. My bitterest regret? Losing my marriage and my family because I was stupid enough to think making money was more important. Yes, of course it is important, but the other stuff isn't something you can expect to wait for you until you have the time.'

Why time is so important

Sharing time together is the way we get closer and feel connected. Doing the little things that make our daily lives, telling each other our thoughts and our feelings – it's through this process that we build bonds.

Key idea: Time helps relationships grow

Time together is to a relationship what water is to a plant. It's how a relationship, whether with a partner, a family member or a friend, is nurtured and cared for. It's the stuff that makes it stronger and helps it to grow. To stay connected as a couple and a family you need to feed your relationship with time. Time to keep in touch with what's happening in your everyday lives. Time to share your hopes and dreams as well as your fears and failings. And time to have fun.

Remember this: Points to consider

▶ When looking at regrets, the most important thing is to recognize what you can or cannot change.

▶ You cannot alter the past but you can deal with any sense of resentment or self-reproach you may feel about it.

▶ The better the life/work balance you can achieve, the more regret-free a life you will likely to have.

Top tips to help you achieve a life/work balance

1 **Acknowledge your life stage.** There will be times in your life when you have even less time than normal – for example when you have very small children, have just started a business or are caring for an elderly relative. There may seem to be little that you can do to change your circumstances in times like these. But acknowledging where you are at and knowing that this is a phase can help you to feel less stressed. It can also help you take some small but significant measures to still make some time for your partner, even if your are under pressure from other demands.

2   **Get help.** If you're going through a particularly demanding time
    in your life, then grab as much help as you possibly can. There
    are a host of technological miracles, from Internet shopping to
    the dishwasher, that can save time. If you can afford it, get a
    cleaner; if not, rope in the family. Bulk cook and freeze some
    meals – rather than buy in ready meals, use cooking together
    as a way of spending time with your children and partner. Ask
    grandparents to do the ironing; ask your sister to babysit. You'd
    do the same for them if the situation were reversed.

3   **Don't be a perfectionist.** Remember that when you're very
    busy it's better to let your standards slip rather than your
    relationship. Your family will judge you by the time you
    spent listening to them and talking with them, not by the
    shine on your floors or the dust bunnies under the bed. Any
    meal tastes better when it's eaten together – remember, you
    can't see the clutter by candlelight.

4   **Schedule couple time.** Lots of people feel it's far too formal
    to schedule time together as a couple. But sometimes making
    an appointment to share time with your partner and your
    family is the only way to make it happen. The method may
    not be romantic or spontaneous, but the outcome could be.

5   **Schedule family time.** Ask children who feel their family is
    struggling what single thing they would like to change and nine
    times out of ten they will say they would love a weekly 'games
    night' – not screen games but good old-fashioned round-the-
    table board games, because they give such opportunity for talk
    and laughter and face-to-face interaction as well as competition.
    Having one night a week when the screens go off and the
    family eat together then play together can have profoundly
    transformational effects on family cohesion and happiness.

6   **Think quality not quantity.** It's a cliché, but it's true. If you only
    have a short period of time to play with, then make every second
    count. Book times when you can talk as well as times when
    you can crash out together on the sofa and watch a film. And
    remember that it's so easy to keep in touch during the day. Get
    into the habit of exchanging text messages, posting on a social
    network site, making a phone call, or meeting for ten minutes in
    a private chat room. Do whatever you can to keep in touch.

7 **Expand your timetable.** If it's simply not possible to fit everything into one week, then consider expanding your timetable. Rather than stressing and ultimately failing to manage that romantic evening, that family games night or that long country walk every week, consider scheduling on a fortnightly or even monthly basis. It may not be ideal, but it may be more realistic and less likely to fail.

8 **Consider your priorities.** If you've tried everything above and you still don't feel you have enough time as a couple or a family, then you may have to have a long hard look at your priorities. Are there activities in your life that you should seriously consider dropping – at least for the time being? Sacrificing something you enjoy doing is always difficult – but are you willing to risk your relationship instead?

Case study: Jamal

'All of us seemed to have so many things we did and couldn't give up – club nights and games practice for the kid and for us too. We suddenly realized we didn't have one night a week when we could all sit down round the table and have a meal together. And it was showing – I felt so out of touch with my wife and children and all we did when we rushed past each other was shout or bicker. So we made ourselves get together and talk it over and we decided we'd rather eat together at least twice a week and drop some of our activities. It made family life so much better that we made more changes so we could have three nights and lunch on Sundays, and then do stuff together afterwards. We didn't miss the things we'd dropped at all.'

What are your regrets about?

Regrets can be about sins of omission or commission – not having made the effort to stay in touch with friends, or having been judgemental and critical so that people have learned to avoid us. Regrets can be about major issues in our lives – about, for instance, getting our work/life balance wrong so we neglect and lose touch with family and friends. Perhaps the main regret reported by people towards the end of their lives is not having kept up the connection with the people they love.

But almost as, if not equally, damaging can be the painful memory of a lost toy in childhood, or a lost opportunity that in hindsight might seem trivial. Self-blame and feelings of failure resulting from minor regrets can be as significant in our lives and hold us back as much as the sadness over the big things. It may appear to trivialize the larger issues if we take as much notice of and care over tackling the small things, but in fact it is worth while considering and dealing with all regrets.

One reason may be that, when we mourn an apparently unimportant aspect in our past, we may really be using that as a cover for something quite important and quite significant. Deirdre, for instance, regretting the loss of her teddy bear, was really mourning the lack of love and security she experienced in childhood and was experiencing again in a bad relationship. Once she was prepared to look back and think about it, she was able to consider and expose her true feelings and so deal with them. She couldn't go back, but she could certainly move forward, and dump the boyfriend who behaved so cavalierly with her emotions.

In later chapters we'll be looking at the skills of thinking about, confronting and changing our attitudes to our past and so our future. You can turn your regrets into inspiration, and we'll look at how.

> 'It is not only what we do but also what we do not do for which we are accountable.'
>
> Molière

Focus points

✳ Being self-aware – looking at what you really want and are doing – is the most effective way of avoiding future regrets.

✳ Lack of confidence or fear of embarrassment or over-consideration of what others might think are often the background or direct cause of regrets.

✳ Learning to differentiate between things we can have power over and those we cannot control is an important skill for a regret-free life.

✳ Developing resilience is the best protection against present and future regrets.

✳ When looking at any regrets, you need a clear recognition of what you can and cannot change,

✳ The past cannot be altered, but how you deal with any resentment or self-reproach can.

✳ Effort put into achieving the best possible life/work balance for you will pay the biggest dividends.

✳ Optimum use of time, particularly shared time with family, friends or partners, is one of the best defences against the onset of regrets.

✳ Recognizing where you are in your life and what are reasonable expectations at this time will help in avoiding regrets.

✳ Prioritize and ask yourself what is best for you now and how this will affect you in the future.

Next step

The next chapter, on family, looks in more detail at the strategies we can use to increase the time we spend with the important people in our lives so that we can avoid future regret.

2

'I wish I had made enough time for my family'

In this chapter you will learn:

▶ *How to recognize and interpret memories of the past or feelings of something 'missing'*

▶ *The importance of making proper time for family, distant family or any other relationships to avoid regrets in the future*

▶ *That couple relationships need special attention*

▶ *The strategies to use now to avoid regret in the future.*

Memories of the past

We all have different regrets that bother us, and we'll soon be looking at, identifying and addressing them. But I don't think it's too sweeping a statement to say that almost everyone shares this regret – 'I wish I had made enough time for my family.' It's probably the number-one regret expressed by people as they get older or even approach the end of their lives; so many of us look back and look around and wish that we had spent more time with our children, our partners or even our wider family.

What we could be mourning is that we don't have happy memories of the past as we would like to have, or see other people enjoying. One respondent to my questionnaire said their regret was 'not coming from a large, loving, close family'. Another said:

> 'My wife talks so fondly of her childhood and the fun she had with her brother and sister – people she still loves and sees often. Or of her parents, who are such lovely people and I can see how supportive and kind they must have been because they still are. And, while I benefit from it, as do our children, sometimes I feel so bitter and angry because that's not what my childhood was like at all. My mother was cold and unapproachable and my father worked abroad and was hardly ever home. When he was, he spent most of the time playing golf with his friends. So I envy her and wish it had been like that for me.'

It may be that what we grieve for is having lost out on significant milestones that might have occurred when we were otherwise engaged. Glen said his regret was:

> 'wasting valuable time doing things that seemed so important but now I realize I missed my children's first steps, first words, first performances and so many, many events when I should have been there to bear witness, to show I loved them, to be part of their lives. I look back and realize I'm on the outside looking in. Every time my teenage son or my adult daughters want to share anything

or ask anything they'll do it with my wife. Not me. I'm a business success but, to be honest, I'm a total failure where it matters most.'

What's missing?

Or it may be that we look around and recognize what has gone missing – contact with people we used to interact with a lot and who were important to us. Maybe they have not lost that importance to us but we have lost that closeness.

'I wish a had a closer relationship with my siblings. We used to fight but no more than most brothers and sisters. We did, however, back each other up and shared a lot. Now we live at opposite ends of the country, it seems. Until our mother died and my dad went into a home we met up at Christmas but even that has gone now. I wish I knew how to turn this around but it seems so hard.'

Family time

Why should it be important to make enough time for your family? Keeping in touch with parents and grandparents may seem a 'no brainer'. Parents are the ones who brought you up, cared for you and launched you into the world. You may have some areas of conflict, but on the whole, in most families, your parents are people you wish to go on seeing and want to have in your children's lives as their grandparents. If you're lucky to have known them and had loving grandparents yourself, you know what an asset they can be to a child's life. It's not just in childcare, but in the passing on of family stories, family jokes, family likes and dislikes, that grandparents come into their own. Knowing and keeping contact with the previous generation gives you a knowledge and an awareness of your roots, and human beings do seem to both need and thrive best when they have some contact with and understanding of who they are and where they came from. Not having that foundation or losing it can produce profound dislocation – a sense of not knowing who you are by not knowing who preceded and gave rise to you.

Try it now: Start a 'memory box'

We all have things that provoke memories – it may be a photograph, an ornament, an article of clothing. Often they are scattered around the house; sometimes they are stuffed into a box in the cupboard under the stairs, and, of course, nowadays they may be online, in the cloud. Next time you and the family are all together, gather a handful of trigger items or fire up your computer or phone and talk through the memories they evoke. Then suggest you begin a 'memory box' – somewhere you consciously keep things that will spark off stories and reminiscences. Everyone should contribute – from the very young to the very old. And contents can be physical items or digital, either on memory sticks or with a note of the links that will lead to them.

THE MORE DISTANT FAMILY

More distant family members – aunts and uncles, cousins, nieces and nephews – may seem to be an optional extra in busy lives. They might have seemed important when you were young – cousins could have been playmates who chimed instantly with you because you already shared certain traits and a family history, and of course uncles and aunts can be the source of treats and birthday and festival presents – so what's not to love? Children often adore listening to their parents and their siblings hash over old family tales, bringing new perspectives and old disagreements to something they've already heard but only from their parents' viewpoint. And it can be reassuring to know that these are adults you can go to with questions and problems, who will respond because they love you and you are linked, but who are slightly more objective about the issues and don't see them as reflecting on their parenting.

But we often lose touch as adults because families move around more often these days and may live a distance apart. Or it may be because family feuds begun by other people may cause splits and schisms. With busy lives, it may seem more important to focus on the people who are near at hand rather than expending energy on those far away. And, of course, friends and new social networks may fill the gap previously filled by aunts and uncles, cousins, nieces and nephews. Human beings have always had friends and valued the relationships they have with people they choose to be close to rather than those born into an association with them. But it would seem in the last few years that friendship has been elevated in importance and friends have become the new family. Maybe it's because, certainly in the developed world, we value individualism and thus choice. And, while you can choose your friends, you can't choose your family. But this begs the question – while you may notice how losing close family members can impoverish you and cause you to lose your roots and thus something valuable to you, does losing touch with wider family members do the same and should we resist the drift?

THE IMMEDIATE FAMILY

When it comes to your immediate family, the loss inherent in lacking close ties with them cannot be denied or understated. Children suffer when a parent is missing from their lives, and this can be true just as much when a parent is not there because they spend long periods away from the home due to work commitments than when a parent is absent as a result of relationship breakdown. But it can also be true where a parent is emotionally and psychologically unavailable. If an adult's mind is for ever on other things when with a child – concentrating on the other adults present, using social media or messaging friends, engrossed in television or games – the child can feel just as rejected as if the adult had left the room or the home entirely.

Key idea: Be available to your children

Your being unavailable is felt by children as proof that they are of no value to you, that they have failed in being worthy of your notice. And that tells them they have no value at all.

You may feel that what you are doing is essential for the family – earning the money they need to buy those trainers, for instance, or giving yourself the chance to relax and refresh. But children don't need *things* as much as they need *you* – your attention, your approval and your interaction. Children who endlessly ask for things – new clothes, now toys, new gadgets – tend to want them not because they want the items themselves, but to be given them as proof of your love. They would thrive better and be more content if they had more of you.

We tend to underestimate the time we spend away or on our devices interacting with people not in the room with us, and what that says to the people around you. Children grow up fast, and partners and other close family members drift away from us unless we make the time to see them. It's not enough to promise – we have to do it. It's not enough to wait for the time to become free; we have to make it so. Of course, we have to work to make the money to pay for our expenses, and of course we also need to pay attention to the other people in our lives. But children would actually rather they had us read them a bedtime story every night and play with them over the weekend than have a long holiday to a Florida theme park once a year or a big car.

Sometimes we have to prioritize our expenses. There is a wonderful song that every parent should listen to, called 'Cat's in the Cradle' by Harry Chapin – look it up on YouTube. It records how a man rejoices in the birth of his son, but 'there were planes to catch and bills to pay' and, as his son grows up without him, he endlessly promises to spend time with him when he has the time. He is forever promising they'll have a good time together when he has the time, always 'then'. Eventually, he's retired and finally has the time, but now it's his son who promises to see him when *he* has the time, and that they'll have a good time, then.

Key idea: Don't put quality time on the back-burner

Put spending time with your family on the backburner, intending to 'catch up' when you feel the time has come, and you are likely to find they have moved on when you do turn to them.

As one of my questionnaire respondents said: 'I regret not talking to my parents more. Looking back, I'm kind of baffled by them, wish I had asked them about themselves when I had the chance.' And another regretted 'not finding out more about my family before my parents died'. But the problem is that the impetus to spend time relaxing and chatting, to be open to questions and happy to share, has to come from the adults. If your parents didn't do it, you will be at a disadvantage with them and may carry on that disadvantage into the way you run your own family. The world is full of children who have little relationship with one or both of their parents because the adults did not make that time to spend with them. A frequent excuse I hear is that the parent was too busy, had too much to juggle and do, and felt it would be OK as long as their children knew that they loved them and that one day they could have the time to spend together.

Sadly, you can't put relationships on a back-burner, to wait until you are ready. It's clearly better if they know you love them, but actually love is not enough. Attention is the way you show love and, without it, that love may feel hollow and devalued, because the child or adult who is neglected feels devalued. And you learn how best by having it done to you. As Glen said: 'It took me years to see I was happiest when I was with my family – spending time with them and putting real effort into being a dad.'

THE COUPLE RELATIONSHIP

It's not only the parent–child relationship that needs nurturing and developing, and having time spent on it. Agony aunts and counsellors also often deal with partners who have neglected to keep their own couple relationship alive because of work commitments or once children arrived. If you do this, once faced with the empty nest as your youngsters leave home, or with retirement or the winding down of work demands, you may find you have nothing left between you.

Again, you can't put having a connection, sharing and spending time together, on the back-burner. Nature abhors a vacuum, so, if your partner is spending time away – however much they may be doing it for you – you'll fill the time with something else. That may simply be spending more time with your own work, or your kids, or your family or your friends or watching television. The point is that the space your partner should have filled becomes filled by something else. And when they come back wanting to be in your life, there's little room and often little inclination because you've grown apart and are now strangers.

Remember this: Points to consider

▶ Most regrets come from unhappy memories of the past or from feelings that something is 'missing' in our lives.

▶ What you can do now – getting insight and making adjustments – will help you get a regret-free future for yourself and others.

▶ Prioritizing and making proper use of time are the two main keys to success – whether you are in a family, in a relationship or on your own.

Making things work for you

So how can you address the way you interact with your immediate and also your distant family? How can you get your work/life balance right and prioritize whom to spend time with and how?

BREAK THE PATTERN

Family closeness often starts when you see and experience the model of how that's done in your own family of origin. If your family is fragmented and people who should have loved you are cold or absent, you can find it difficult to act differently as you grow up because you don't have a model to follow. You have to break the pattern. Some people, such as Glen, chose partners who came from families that were warm and loving and he eventually took that as his model. He looked at what he might have preferred for himself, and gave that to his partner and children. In doing so, he found it didn't just benefit them but him as well. Sometimes you can break the pattern by communicating with those around you and working towards what you might have liked and would like now. Sometimes you need help to do so, with the professional guidance of organizations such as Family Lives or Relate (see Appendix).

LEARN TO PRIORITIZE

It's very easy to fall into the habit of responding to the immediate calls on your time, or to whoever shouts loudest. Whether it's running around after the children because they need you most, or staying on the phone with a family member or friend because they want to talk, or taking the extra work or overtime or promotion because it's offered and we feel we could do with the money... sometimes we need to take a step back and consider whether the things we're not doing because of all those pressures might in fact be more important. The question to ask is: in the long run, which of these would really benefit me and my family best, and which simply fill my time? Is the cleaning more important than having some shared time and shared fun with the people you love and value? Is your work more important than your life? What might you be missing out, and what might you gain if you shifted your priorities?

Key idea: Think about what's valuable

Frequently, we cite the need to earn money as a reason for spending more time at work than with family – the need to do extra work to keep up in a career path or to do overtime. What are you buying with the extra money? Most of the time it's making amends for your absence. Wouldn't your presence with the people you love be more valuable?

LEARN TO SHARE

If you are looking at priorities, one important aspect might be to consider who does what and how you manage the responsibilities in your life. Sit down with your partner and your children and look at the things that need doing to run your house and life – cooking, cleaning, shopping, earning money, etc., etc. When one person takes on an unfair burden, it affects the way you can relate to one another. Working women, too, often take on the lion's share at home, either because they feel they have to prove they are still 'real' women who can be perfect wives and mothers as well as work, or because everyone else around them assumes that it's women's and mother's work and not their responsibility as well.

The often inevitable outcome is that, while the dusting and ironing may not suffer, everything else does. Taking full or major responsibility for what goes to make a house run smoothly on top of paid work is exhausting – you seldom have time or the energy to talk, play and enjoy being with your family as well. And it can build resentment, as one person rushes around cooking, cleaning and making arrangements while the others consider this to be their 'downtime' to be spent doing things they choose. If you want to share enjoyable time with your partner and family, the first stage is also to share the necessary routines and tasks. That may require you recognizing the need to share, and forging ways and agreements to do so.

LEARN TO LET GO

Sometimes it simply doesn't matter if the dust bunnies gather under the bed or the underwear does not get ironed. Neither does it matter who does what. What we often need to let go of is the image that we might have of what makes the perfect woman or man, partner, wife or husband, mum or dad. Being a perfect dad isn't always being the one in charge or the one earning the money or the one doing the telling-off. It can be the one changing nappies, taking time off to take a child to the doctor, the one buying flowers or making cupcakes. Being a perfect woman doesn't mean having it all, juggling home and work seamlessly so that no one sees the gaps. It can mean being the one who stops doing the laundry to play, talk and listen or simply hang out with the family. Listen to that small voice that tells you that you 'ought' to be doing this and 'should' be doing that, if you want to be that stereotypical woman or man, partner, wife or husband, mum or dad. Then tell it to shut up, and go and do what you know is right for the moment.

LEARN TO BE REALISTIC

You may have an idea of what you want from your partner or family and what you feel able to put in, but the rules and the expectations can elude you.

> 'I married too young to someone I later realized I hardly knew. I had a sort of fantasy image of what she should be and by the time I could see she wasn't that at all, it was too late. I had three kids because I so wanted that wonderful, noisy, happy, loving family I saw on TV. It so wasn't like that!'

In reality, you can't 'have it all' if by that you mean being able to work to your maximum, play to your maximum and look after everyone else in your life to your maximum. The people who seem to be doing so cheat – they either have staff who actually do most of the routine work for them or they are short-changing the people closest to them. Being realistic means recognizing that something has to give and everyone has to muck in for you all to achieve most of what you all want.

Social media

Isn't digital media wonderful? Isn't it such a boon that we now have powerful, often inexpensive, handheld or portable and widely available devices that can entertain, inform us and keep us in touch?

However, when it comes to family cohesion, electronic media in the home can be seen as not only one of the most powerful but also one of the most pernicious influences on family ties. It can bring you together and reinforce bonds, but in some cases and in some situations the time both adults and children spend on screen is not only coming between them, reducing connection and intimacy, but is actually harming their ability to connect.

Key idea: Virtual friendships can be a substitute for intimacy

Connection is wonderful, and using social media to connect can be beneficial. But it is one step removed from touchy-feely, face-to-face, meet-my-eyes-and-get-to-know-me contact and, as such, is sometimes used as a way of avoiding real intimacy. As an *addition* – it's great. As *substitute*… it's worrying.

Friends on Facebook or people you message and access through any other social medium may be the people you also see face to face and with whom you have real-world relationships. They may be people you know but who live some distance from you. And they can be people you've actually never met, but with whom you have developed friendships through this particular medium. And I would never discount the importance of any of that. It can be wonderful to be able to keep up a dialogue and a connection with your friends and family in a quick and easy way, and in a forum where lots of you can take part at the same time. That's fine with people you see regularly but can be even more satisfying when it's with people you might otherwise lose touch with because they live at a distance. And, of course, the Internet has allowed us the ability to search for people we might otherwise have lost touch with or to find new friends.

> 'I joined a recipe club a few years ago and met some like-minded people through that. It actually folded but a few of us formed an online chat group, and brought in some other friends and it's developed and developed. I "talk" daily with people in the United States, Canada, Australia, Argentina, the Philippines and South Africa as well as the UK – it's brilliant. And I've met a few of them face to face, too. They're real friends and I'm so grateful for having had the opportunity to know them. Which doesn't in any way detract from the face-to-face friends I also have, some of whom have "met" these people on Facebook.'

The opportunities social media offer cannot be underestimated. But it's really important to recognize that, just because you *can*, doesn't mean you always *should*. And that making time for the people you are with should take precedence over answering messages and sending your own.

Key idea: Keeping up your real-life connections

Get into the habit of going your different ways once you get home and very soon you'll have lost the habit of spending time together. And that is the one-way trip to realizing when it might be too late that you have lost touch and lost the ability to feel comfortable in each other's company and when communicating with each other.

It's very easy to fall into the trap of feeling that letting children have access to information and entertainment in their own rooms stops conflict. If your children squabble over which programme they want to watch with each other, or you, or simply squabble, you may feel that giving them their own devices stops the arguments. It may – but it also stops the communication. And it stops them ever having to learn how to negotiate, compromise or live together. And the reality is that you cannot keep any control of what young people access when they have devices in their room. Unsuitable material can be found via any Internet-enabled machine – games console and phone as well as computer. Not only is this about what they can see but till what hour – young people need more sleep than they realize and their chances in life can be seriously affected if they are up till all hours on their devices.

Self-assessment: Do you use social media wisely?

Read the following statements and think about whether any of then apply to you:

1 'The first thing I do when I get home is check my messages.'

YES/NO

2 'I never turn off my mobile.'

YES/NO

3 'I and/or my partner take a phone or laptop/netbook/tablet to bed.'

YES/NO

4 'My children have TVs games consoles, computers or other electronic media in their bedrooms.'

YES/NO

5 'My partner and I often spend separate time in the evening or when one of us has gone to bed on electronic media.'

YES/NO

6 'I check messages during the time I am with my partner/family.'

YES/NO

7 'I'm proud of the number of "friends" I have on Facebook.'

YES/NO

8 'We often tweet or update Facebook during the time we are together.'

YES/NO

If you have answered yes to any of these, it's time to consider how much your use of electronic media might be coming between you and your family.

USING SOCIAL MEDIA BENEFICIALLY

We may need to reassess how we use social media. A surprising number of people fall prey to scams on Facebook and the Internet because they don't recognize how many people can see the information we have inputted, and how it can be used. And, if we don't recognize the pitfalls for ourselves, we certainly don't for our children, who are often far more extensive, but no more savvy, users than ourselves. Sixty-two per cent of 12- to 15-year-olds own a smartphone, and a significant number of them browse the Net and use their phone at the same time as watching television. And one-third of children have no parental control on the Internet function on those phones.

Young people can access pornography that is far more explicit, as well as being far more accessible, than anything their parents might have been able to see when they were that age. A really worrying percentage of teenagers are growing up thinking that the exploitative, violent and anti-women relationships that they see in online pornography – which is sometimes their first introduction to sexual matters – is what sex is all about. As a result, online bullying has increased, as has 'sexting' – sending sexually explicit texts or pictures. The answer is not to avoid the situation but to take control of it. Gaming, television programmes and social media can all be very pleasant additions to our lives, but the more we control them and use them in a way that adds to, rather than detracts from, the quality of our relationships, the better.

TIPS FOR ELECTRONIC MEDIA

▶ Make a rule – **all mobiles off** as people come in the door – so you can all touch base when you see each other instead of having to fight for attention. Have a shelf or bowl in the hall or kitchen where they are parked. And that applies to *everyone*...

▶ Kids can multi-task – do homework, check mobile and Internet messages, listen to music. That's fine, but **no multi-tasking while you are having 'family time'** – catching up when everyone has just got home, over a meal or while sharing time together afterwards.

▶ Allow people to check messages and update but **prioritize face-to-face contact**. That applies to *everyone*...

- **Place computers, TVs and games consoles in common areas** – in the living room or kitchen, or in a room overlooked by the living room or kitchen. If you do feel you can trust your child to have a computer in their room, discuss rules for this and make it clear you'll be checking which sites they've been visiting as a condition of their being able to have access.

- **Agree sanctions** if rules are broken.

- **Regularly check 'browser history'** – apply a sanction if the browser history has been cleared and if websites you've said are off limits have been accessed.

- **Set limits on how much screen time** you'll all have each night. Ban all electronic media use in bedrooms after bedtime. Enforce a 'screens off' rule at least half an hour before bedtime.

- **Discuss what programmes people want to watch and come to an agreement.** Negotiate, compromise, use time-shifting or recording to manage clashes.

- **Discuss with your children** what they watch, what games they play and how they use social media.

- **Ideas-storm other things to do together** – board game nights, visits to the park, a 'making things night', a 'chat around the evening meal table night'...

Having come to some understanding, make the decision to take control. Rather than continuing to mourn the past, make excuses or procrastinate about change, look at ways of grasping the nettle and taking action.

Your Action Plan: Step 1 – identify your main regrets

So how are you going to do your best to stave off those regrets in later life, or deal with the ones you already have? If you want to make enough time for your family now and in the future, and redress any losses from your past, how do you go about it?

Step one in your Action Plan will be to determine what your main regret may be. Is it something you did or something you didn't do? Something someone else did or did not do?

Something beyond your control, or that you could have done differently? Often our feelings of guilt or sadness stop us actually putting our finger on what we regret, and if you don't know what it is, you can't fix it.

You could do this on your own or with someone you trust such as your partner, a family member or friend. One good technique to find your way to an understanding is to 'ideas-storm'.

Try it now: Arrange an 'ideas-storming' session

Ideas-storming is a technique for working out what is the problem at hand. You also ideas-storm to find a solution that works, but, on that, more later. You start off sitting at a table with paper and pens at hand. If you're doing this on your own, you could sit somewhere comfortable with a laptop, netbook or tablet on your lap to make the necessary notes, but if you are sharing the exercise with anyone else, you want each person to feel they are part of this, on an equal footing and focusing on the issue at hand. If only one or a few people can see the screen and people are slumped around a sitting room on chairs, sofas or the floor, it's easy for them to get distracted or feel left out.

Ask the question. It might be: Do you have regrets or do you think you might have regrets later in life and what might they be? (See the list below for other ideas for questions.) It is important to be clear about the issue. If you are vague or contradictory, you may find it harder to reach a real understanding of your feelings or a resolution. It helps to set your mind on being positive and creative – this is not a blaming or fault-finding exercise, although it might be important to recognize where responsibility lies. It's about clarifying in order to make the situation better.

The key to successful ideas-storming is that initially you put down everything that pops into your mind, no matter how trivial or silly it seems. Often, a small regret over an inconsequential issue is the tip of an iceberg that is actually deep, wide, large and important. Remember Deirdre and her teddy bear, which represented the love and security she never felt she had in her childhood and which she didn't feel at the time in her relationship. It was only when she acknowledged how upset she felt over the loss that she could see that her regret was not so much at losing the bear but what it represented – her feeling that she never got what she needed, either from her parents or that boyfriend. Finally recognizing it led to her being able to do something about it.

If you are doing the ideas-storming with other people, one of you should function as a recorder and a facilitator, welcoming all ideas but holding off discussion of them until later. Once you have your list, think or talk them over – what was this about, why, when and how? Simply thinking or talking them over can in itself be liberating and lead to insights.

The questions I asked in my questionnaire might help you. They were:

* Most people say they can look back and regret some aspects of their lives. What would you say are your own top five regrets? Feel free to explain in detail. If you've more than five, do describe them all!
* For some people, regrets are about things they have done; for others, it's about the things not done. What would you say is true for you, and in what way?
* If you could go back, what would you change or wish had been different?
* Do you think the things you regret have made a big difference to your life now, and in what way?
* What do you think may have been different about your life if you had not done, or had done, the things you have regretted?
* Do you have any particular regrets about your childhood or teens?
* Do you have any particular regrets about your twenties or thirties?
* Do you have any particular regrets about your forties or fifties or later?
* If you have children, do you have any regrets about anything you did or did not do in their childhood, teenage or adult years?
* If you could go back, what advice would you have for your younger self, to avoid your regrets?

Key idea: Do a warm-up

You can 'warm up' for an ideas storm, and, incidentally, see how effective it can be, by asking your group how many uses they can find for a drinking straw, or a button or a DVD disc. Try it – you'll be surprised!

Case study: Dan

Nearing the magic age of 40, Dan had found himself becoming more and more snappy and moody. He couldn't explain what it was that was making him so frustrated and upset so his partner, Alice, finally suggested they had an ideas storm with their teenage children. Asking the question 'What's upsetting Dad?' they finally reached a conclusion. Coming up to middle age, he'd never fulfilled his ambition of hitching to Kathmandu. He'd dismissed it as impractical – a teenage dream that got lost when he left university and started a family. With small children he and his wife needed to holiday nearer to home; the furthest they'd ever been on holiday was Florida. But the whole family applauded the idea of being more adventurous. Kathmandu might have to wait until the children left home but, for now, they bought and did up a camper van, and the following summer spent an entire month wandering around Eastern Europe, finding places to stay as they went along.

The key to ideas-storming is that, hidden among all the trivia and jokes, the silly ideas and the memories, you are likely to be able to put your finger on what it is that is bothering you. Dig a little deeper among the niggles from the past and you may be able to unearth the one thing, or several things, that are holding you back and which you'd like to redress or change.

Once you have a list – you don't at this point have to reduce or prioritize the number of items – divide it into two categories: issues you could have done something about and issues that would have been beyond your control. This can be harder than it seems. The truth is that we do often blame ourselves or feel guilty about issues that actually are nothing to do with us. The regret may arise primarily because we felt responsible – because we felt that if we had done something differently a situation might not have happened. Realizing that it wasn't up to you to make that choice at that time can, in itself, lessen the feelings of unhappiness. Seth said:

> *'I've felt guilty for years about the fact that I never used a present my grandmother – whom I adored – gave me when I was eight. She lived abroad and gave me a year's*

*membership to a theatre company that did wonderful
shows for kids. I never went and I felt I'd let her down,
for ages. I've now got kids of my own and Gran has been
gone for decades, but just a few years ago it suddenly
came to me that I can't blame myself – I was eight, for
God's sake! Why didn't my mum take me? Well, I know
why – she and my gran didn't get on. So that was pretty
mean of her, but the main thing was to realize that I
didn't have to feel bad any more – it wasn't my fault her
gift was wasted.'*

Issues beyond your control, then, might be regrets about what
happened to you in your family because of other people's
actions or beliefs. Stan, for instance, said:

*'My parents divorced when I was a baby and my mother
avoided talking about my father. There were a few
remarks and stories she'd tell but if I asked any questions
the shutters would come down. When I finally said I
felt it was unfair and I wanted to know more, she said
he'd hurt her and she didn't want to talk about him, and
that was that. My feelings or needs in the matter simply
didn't figure. Years later I traced him, but I'd missed him
by several years and he was dead. I always regret that I
didn't meet him and get his side of the story. Even if I
had decided I'd support my mother against him, I still
wish I'd had the chance to know more about him – he
was my dad.'*

And a respondent to my questionnaire said she was sad 'that my
mother died before she could see her grandchildren'.

Neither of these things would actually have been in their power
to alter at the time. However much you might have fretted
and even obsessed about the situation, if the reality was that
you could have not have changed it, that in itself is a relief
to realize. It was out of your hands, so there's no point in
continuing to beat yourself up about the fact it happened. It
often helps to know when something was beyond your control.
There may equally be no point in blaming the other people
involved. Parents, or friends or other people in your life who
let you down may likewise have been unable at the time to act

differently. That doesn't mean to say that you have to shrug and decide that no one need take responsibility for what happened, but it does mean that considering the situation may help you to come towards some forgiveness of their actions, however much you felt they harmed you.

Regrets such as

> 'I regret not calling my dad back when I was going away and him dying before I returned – I feel like I didn't tell him I loved him that one last time'

> 'I regret not keeping some of my children's clothes – the special crocodile PJs or the cherry dress' or

> 'I regret that I didn't say thank you enough'

on the other hand, might have been something that you could have done differently.

This isn't to say that those issues that were beyond your control then are beyond your control now. You may not be able to go back and change them, but you can certainly act to make yourself feel better about them, and minimize their effect on you now. And recognizing what regrets might have been caused by an action or inaction of your own really can set you on the road to changing your behaviour now and in the future. Making a promise to yourself to speak up to the people you love or keep mementos in future can help.

Try it now: What might have gone into the memory box?

If you've started that memory box, it's a helpful exercise to look back and think of the things that you might have liked to have put in it – old mementoes now lost or photographs never taken. Keeping a note of them may not be quite the same thing as the item itself – but it still serves to recall the memory when you sift through your memory box.

Remember this: Points to consider

▶ To break the pattern of inherited, present or future regrets, you need to prioritize, share and learn to let go.

▶ You also need to be realistic because so many regrets are based on unrealistic expectations.

▶ By ideas-storming, you should be able to find something that will help you get rid of any of the unnecessary regrets that trouble you.

Top tips for being regret free

▶ **Have some routines.** Being spontaneous and impulsive is sometimes an excellent thing – throwing caution to the winds and choosing a day out instead of cleaning the home! But it also really helps to have some routines you stick to such as family mealtimes and bedtimes. And one of the most important is to…

▶ **Wake up and smell the coffee.** We tend to feel a lie-in on days off can refresh and revitalize us. In fact, you're much better off getting up at the same time every morning, whether on days off or holidays, and going to bed early if you need extra sleep.

▶ **Break bread together.** There are plenty of reasons to both cook and eat together, as a family and as friends. For a start, a healthy diet contributes to your physical and emotional wellbeing. Food cooked from scratch is not only cheaper and better for you, but it allows you the really valuable interaction of making meals together, giving you a sense of confidence and achievement. Children who share meal preparation are infinitely less likely to be faddy eaters. And families or couples who eat round a table are likely to be closer, have less conflict and fewer areas of disagreement.

▶ **Smell the roses.** Spending too much time looking back, or anticipating the future, prevents you enjoying the present. It really helps to 'be in the moment' as often as possible, recognizing what is around you and taking pleasure from it.

▶ **Choose your battles.** It's become a cliché, but it is also true, that you should accept the things you cannot change, have the courage to change the things you can, and cultivate the wisdom to know the difference.

'People will forget what you said and what you did but will never forget how you made them feel.'

Maya Angelou

Focus points

✳ By recognizing and interpreting what may have happened in the past, you can deal with many present feelings of regret.

✳ Understanding what you feel is 'missing' in your life and making adjustments can be a good way of not perpetuating current regrets.

✳ Making enough time for family, or any other relationship, can stop them having their own regrets in the future.

✳ There is always time or opportunity to change your feelings about the past and to plan the future so that regrets do not continue or damage others.

✳ With the right self-knowledge and insight, you can be your own future.

✳ A surprising amount is in your control – all that is needed to make things work for you are some well-thought-out prioritizing and proper use of your time.

✳ Social media is not always a good thing – it can be divisive as well as bringing people together.

✳ Make social media work for you – it can be a marvellous way of keeping in touch with friends and family near and far.

✳ Regular meals around a table together could be the best step you have taken towards a regret-free life for all of you.

✳ The top tips to be learned by heart are: 'Choose your battles', 'Wake up and smell the coffee', 'Smell the roses' – and 'Become regret-free!'

Next step

In the next chapter, on friendship, you will learn how to find and build supportive networks of friends and how to identify potential friendship problems so that you can avoid them before they arise.

3

'I wish I had kept in touch with my friends'

In this chapter you will learn:

- ► *Why you need, and how to find, support networks*
- ► *How to look for and find friends*
- ► *What can complicate friendships*
- ► *Why friendships break up and how to avoid this happening.*

The support network

We all need a support network – that web of best friends, good friends, neighbours and acquaintances, colleagues and employees – to make life manageable and enjoyable. To some we go to have fun – a drink, a coffee, a night out. Some we pay to do the essential things with which we need help – a babysitter, a child-minder or carer, a cleaner. Others feed the cat or keep an eye on our home when we're away; with others we merely exchange pleasantries in passing. There are different levels of give and take and intimacy – with some you share your problems and ask for advice or support, and it's not always with the ones with whom you are most intimate that you do that. You may choose to share more with your hairdresser or your neighbour than with your best friends, mainly because you see them less and so you can spill the problem and then put it behind you.

But all these relationships share the same thing – you have to offer reciprocal actions to keep them going. Friendships need 'servicing' just like a car. Instead of the occasional oil change, what a friendship needs is a frequent dose of coffee, chat and sympathy if we're all to receive help when we need it – and for us to get the fun and laughter we also deserve from our friendships. But it also has to be an equal exchange for it to be a good and functioning friendship. Gita comments:

> 'I had three friends when I left school and we used to meet up for a drink once a month. After a year I realized that, if I didn't suggest it, we wouldn't get together. And my boyfriend pointed out to me that the two of them were always on the phone asking for advice and spilling out their problems to me, but whenever I needed a shoulder to cry on they were too busy. So I stopped asking and we stopped meeting and actually I realized I was better off on the whole. One of them made the effort to get in touch with me and now we're really good friends – she supports me and I support her and we call each other every other day and meet up, with a few other people, at least once a month.'

Family frequently are your support network, too, but to a certain extent we expect the reciprocal nature to be less in evidence. With good friendships, if someone offers you a confidence you feel better if you can give one back, and, if someone asks you for help, sooner or later you will ask them for help, too. If one of you is always asking and the other always helping, two things tend to happen. One is that the helper can begin to feel resentful and used. Everyone needs support at some time but if you're always cast as the one to give the help that means you can't get your own support, and you can feel tired of always having to be the one to come up with the solutions. On the other hand, the person always asking for help can feel more and more incompetent and incapable and that in itself breeds resentment and distress.

You may not realize that this sort of exchange is going on, but in good friendships it happens subtly, in the background, and it's what makes them good. And, if you look at those relationships that feel wrong or burdensome or awkward, often it's because this balance is not there. When we get help from a professional – a counsellor, doctor, dentist or hairdresser – the exchange is in payment. A fee (or our tax dollars!) goes to them; the service comes to us. With friends it's a barter – we offer each other equal help and trust and enjoyment. With family, of course, it is the same, although we might not expect immediate returns. We all help each other, knowing reciprocal help is there for us when we need it. Consider how resentment and arguments can arise in a family when this unacknowledged agreement is broken – the relation who always demands help but never gives it, the one who expects to be part of the festivities but doesn't enter into the spirit.

Why are support networks so important? Nobody can do it on their own. When times are good we need people to share our fortune and with whom to celebrate. When times are difficult we need people to help us, in small or big ways. When times are really tough we need people around us who can sympathize, mobilize and support us, whether it's to find solutions or simply to be there for us. It's all very well being the stoic, strong, capable superman or wonder woman who can manage on their own, but the reality is that most of us could do with some help, in good times and bad.

> **Key idea:** Humans are social beings
>
> Some people may prefer their own company and manage perfectly well on their own. However, most of us want to be in touch and function better when we have the support of our network of friends and contacts.

Finding and building a support network

So how do we find and build our essential support networks? Below are some key tips:

- **Go looking for friends.** People won't beat a path to your door. To make friends you have to put yourself out there. If you have a busy life and meet lots of people, you need to be on the lookout among them for the like-minded individuals with whom you'd want to spend time. If you don't have many chances for social contact, you have to make them. It's an old cliché but it's true that joining clubs, classes or volunteering allows you the opportunity to meet people and make friends.

- **Be welcoming.** It's not enough to be in the places where there are other people – you need to be open and warm to allow them make an approach, or to do it yourself. Sitting with a downcast face and not making eye contact is as bad as not being there at all.

- **Accept the variety.** Friendships come in different sizes and shapes. One person may be the perfect companion on a shopping trip, but send you bonkers if you had to spend a week with them on holiday. Another may be the one you go to for a quiet, reflective coffee or for advice, but not the person you'd choose for a night out on the town. The trick is to recognize that none of us can be all things to all people but that we can offer and accept different things at different times. A variety of friends can reflect all the facets of our own personality, our lives and our needs.

Try it now: Make a list of your friends

Make a list of all your friends and of all the things you might do with them – a night out, a quiet coffee, a walk in the countryside, a shopping trip, a week abroad, etc. Then put your friends in the categories – some may go in several, some only in one. Recognize that all friendships are valid but that it sometimes helps to realize you'd be straining a friendship if you try to fit a friend into a category that doesn't match what they can best offer you, and you them.

▸ **Keep old friends but make new ones.** There's something particularly comforting about an old friend – someone whom you've known for ages, who has seen you grow up and is comfortable with your shared history. But we all change and we meet new people. Rather than discard the old for the new, or shy away from discoveries, you can balance the two. Having one kind of friend does not mean you can't have the other, and they don't have to be seen at the same time.

▸ **Keep in touch.** But here's the crux of it: friendships, whether old or new, need to be maintained. If you want to keep friends, you have to speak to them, communicate with them, spend time with them. The delicate choice we all have to make is how to prioritize the demands on our time, balancing time spent on our partners, children, family and friends as well as on work, housework and all the other calls on our attention. Too much on one facet of our lives and other facets suffer. Not enough on one facet and that suffers.

Case study: Toni

'I lost one friend because I didn't feel it right to lean on her when I got ill. My family were supportive and so were a couple of friends I told about it, but this one friend, because she'd always been someone I helped out, I sort of kept quiet about it to her. I think I thought she'd not be able to cope. Anyway, she eventually found out and she told me she was really hurt, and stopped calling. I don't think it was because it was beyond her; I think it was because I'd stopped her having the chance to pay back. We see each other from time to time but it's never been the same. She never comes to me for help now.'

Try it now: Analyse your circle

One good way of deciding how to apportion time and attention is to do a bull's-eye analysis.

1 Draw a bull's-eye – a series of concentric circles.
2 Put yourself at the centre.
3 Put your very nearest and dearest in the next circle.
4 Work gradually outwards, 'ranking' the people you know according to their importance to you. (How close they actually live to you and how often you see them may be at variance to the importance you place on them.)

How often have you neglected someone really close to you who wants your attention because someone else – someone in a more distant circle – has demanded your notice by calling, texting, posting to or messaging you? How many times has a loved one complained because you weren't there for them, when the reality was that you were concentrated on someone less important, but who shouted louder? Keeping the bull's-eye in mind can help you recognize when you're responding to people who shout the loudest rather than recognizing your true responsibilities.

▶ **Be a good friend.** Do as you would be done by might be the best motto here. If you want good friends, you need to be a good friend – someone who is there when needed to help and support, there when wanted to have fun and celebrate, who gives as much and asks as much as the other. If you're always the helper, you can make your friends feel inadequate; if you're always the demander, you can make them feel used and weary. Being a good friend means being appropriate – people don't thrive as friends when they feel you're never there for them, but neither do they feel comfortable if they realize your partner or children have to wait in line while they have your time.

▶ **Share good and bad.** Being a friend means sharing your tough times as well as your good times. It means trusting your friends to be able to hold you up when you need it, and giving them the joy of celebrating with you when you can.

▶ **Accept help.** We all need support networks. If you don't have one, you need to go out and find one; and if you find making friends difficult, it's a skill you could, and should, ask for help to acquire. You could brush up on skills via reading – my book Teach Yourself *Be More Assertive* could help – or seek the support of organizations such as Relate or Family Lives (see Appendix).

Online friendships

Thanks to Facebook and Twitter, and many other forms of digital connection on multiple platforms, people can now connect, reconnect and continue to connect in ways other than face to face, by letter or on the phone.

ONLINE'S UPSIDE

Online access can be an absolute boon. It allows you to get back in touch with people with whom you may have lost touch. By using social media, or simply by mailing or messaging people you know, you can contact old friends and family members, start a conversation and kick-start your reconnection with them. You can also use it to make new contacts, perhaps by joining online groups that interest you or by striking up conversations with friends of friends. And it's an excellent way to *maintain* friendships. In a busy life you may not have the time to have regular long conversations with people outside your immediate circle, but would like to let them know that you are thinking of them. Sending them a message or 'sharing' something that you've seen online that amuses you or you think will interest them can achieve that.

> '*I'm on a couple of social media sites – one more for social use and one for professional – and I find them really useful. I probably look at my social one half a dozen times a day and I'm trading jokes and videos with people I see regularly as well as some friends I only know online, and some relatives who live on the other side of the world. It keeps me amused and I often have stuff to talk about with friends and family from it. And it keeps me in touch with people I'd otherwise only see at weddings and funerals. And it's given me some friends I'd otherwise never have met. Next year I'm going to Australia, somewhere I've always wanted to go. I'm not sure we would have had the courage to go that*

far if it hadn't been for the fact that I have a dear friend I've known for almost ten years whom I met online. I'll see her face to face for the first time when we arrive, but I have no doubt she, and our holiday, will be as brilliant as I hope!'

Key idea: A communication method that's well adapted to modern life...

One advantage of online communication is that it can keep a conversation going which might be difficult in any other way. A phone call requires both of you to be free at the same moment and to have the time, and even now phone calls can be expensive if overseas. Online contact can also allow you to meet and get to know someone quite well before you meet them face to face.

ONLINE'S DOWNSIDE

There is, however, a serious downside to online use and it's something you need to consider when thinking about keeping in touch with friends. It can be a brilliant addition to your social life. It helps you get back in touch and keep friendships on the boil. It may also allow you to find new people. But if you only ever, or mainly, interact with people online, you are missing out.

One aspect of an online conversation is that it can be superficial – short, limited and without the nuances that you get when you can hear a voice and see a face. That can mean that you get into arguments because you can't hear amusement or irony, and someone may take things the wrong way. But it also means that you may not be able to get to converse very deeply and thus the friendship remains on a surface level. Trading funny cat videos is no substitute for an in-depth dissection of the news of the day, with all your opinions and views. You could do that online, of course, but we seldom do.

If you get hooked on the ease of a friendship at a distance and at the tap of a screen, you can find yourself avoiding the somewhat harder and messier business of interacting with real people in real time. And just like pigeons trained to peck at corn at the ring of a bell, we can find ourselves jumping to the sound of a message arriving – to the detriment of our relationships with the real people in our kitchen, workplace or even in bed with us. When you see a group of people having coffee together but every single one of them manipulating their smartphones, you might look at this either as an admirable example of multi-tasking or as a sad example of dislocation. And what about the family in the living room, where everyone is watching a big screen while also engaged in a small one? In both cases, lots of conversation may be going on with people outside the room, but how much, one wonders, is with the people inside it?

Despite all the opportunities we have to meet up, make friends and keep in touch, I get just as many, if not more, letters from people who are lonely – who feel they have no or few friends, or have lost touch with the friends they used to have – as I did before the digital age. And I am getting an increasing number of letters from families who feel that digital media is coming between them, not helping them.

Key idea: Agree some rules for using digital technology

It can help to use online and digital technology to keep in touch, but once home with your own family it might be a good idea to discuss and agree some rules for how much time you spend communicating with other people. See Chapter 2 for some ideas.

Recurrent problems in friendships and how to deal with them

So what might be your problems about friendships, and how can you overcome them so you don't have to say later in life that you wish you'd kept in touch with your friends? Let's look at some of the commonest problems.

'I'M SO BUSY I CAN'T KEEP IN TOUCH – I CAN'T DO IT ALL'

This is the number-one problem and usually the reason we lose touch with friends. We do all have busy lives and it's perfectly right that partners and immediate family – and, of course, work! – should take precedence. But friendships are also vital because they are something of your own. Your individual friendships allow you down time for yourself – they are the ultimate in 'me time' which everyone should have. Couple friendships are equally important because they give both of you shared time off from being a parent and help strengthen your own bonds.

What should you do? The best tip is to prioritize, recognizing that, while immediate bonds have first call, the second layer of friendships also needs to be allotted time. A few emails or messages daily, a couple of calls a week, meeting for coffee or a meal every month are possible even in a busy life if you recognize the importance of a friendship to you.

'I RESENT MY FRIEND BECAUSE IT ALL SEEMS ONE-SIDED'

Sometimes the one-sidedness is your own responsibility – where you ask for support without offering the same or, more often, where you've become the shoulder to cry on and don't ask for help yourself. Sometimes it is because your 'friend' either is someone who takes more than they give, or who has got into the habit of doing so.

What should you do? To keep friendships alive and thriving we need to make conscious efforts to be reciprocal – to give and take in equal measure. And when we feel someone else is taking advantage, simply stop saying yes and going along with it. See below for how to do that.

'I FEEL WORSE WHEN I'VE SEEN A PARTICULAR FRIEND'

Sometimes the inequality is because one person is the one to always say when and where you meet, or the one to call up and keep you on the phone even though you are busy. And sometimes it's because one person you've accepted as a friend is simply toxic to you – someone who demands more than you can give or is critical or unpleasant. I could say that they have problems of their own and perhaps with sympathy and direction they could become more acceptable. Or I could say that it's not your job to help them do this but to protect yourself and your family, and learn to say no. Part of keeping in touch with friends is knowing when you have to stop being in touch with some of them.

What should you do? A frequent complaint I hear is that someone made you do something – kept you on the phone, for example, or wouldn't let you refuse an invitation, insisting that you went with them or stayed with them. 'She rings me at work and won't get off the phone even though I tell her I'm busy' or 'He calls when we've got a night out planned and then turns up even though we don't want him there.' That's when you need to learn how to say no – our next topic.

'I DON'T SAY NO'

Sometimes you have to take a long hard look at how you contribute to a situation you say you don't like. How does someone keep you on the phone when they ring and you don't want to talk to them? Is your hand and ear glued to the receiver? No – you make the choice to keep on listening and answering. And how do they find out where you are going out for the night? Are they telepathic? No, you tell them. I'm not pretending it's easy to resist when someone has the front to ignore the fact that you are clearly unwelcoming, but the reality is it's your responsibility not to be drawn in.

What should you do? When someone rings you when it's not convenient, simply say 'I can't talk now – I'm busy' and put the phone down. If you are scared of hurting feelings or being rude, remember that someone who demands your attention when you make it clear you can't give it is being insensitive and discourteous and that you have no reason to respond. And, if they try to join you on a social occasion when you don't want them to, remind yourself that they have no right to demand information from you. Cut them off before they even ask by saying: 'Must go, bye!' and put the phone down. Where you go wrong is in feeling that, because someone demands something of you, you have to provide it, whether it's a listening ear or the details of your night out. *You don't*. You can refuse and do so without having to give an explanation. An excuse or an explanation implies they have some call on you – give that and all it does is delay the demand and postpone it to another time. If you don't want to be involved, a simple no is all you owe them.

'WE USED TO HAVE SO MUCH IN COMMON'

Friendships can go out of date. Maybe you shared time with them, and your tastes were in agreement, but as time has passed you've gone different ways and now find you have little in common. I do hear from people who stop being in touch with friends from their past for this reason – they just don't feel they have a link any more. And in some cases I agree. There's no point in flogging dead horses and continuing trying to meet and talk when you actually have nothing to say to each other. However, a note of warning here: you don't want to look back and regret lost friendships. Having different tastes and experiences can be the best foundation for a good relationship. Each of you can bring something new and fresh to your interactions – new ideas for the other to try, new insights into things and ideas you've never encountered.

What should you do? It may be helpful to recognize that you're starting again. Instead of going with the old expectations of the person you once knew, look at them anew with fresh eyes, anticipating something different instead of the 'same old, same old'. Finding you've drifted apart can be the impetus to refresh and renew. What you retain is trust and familiarity, and that's the hardest part of a friendship to build. If you've already got it, it seems a shame to throw it away.

'GOSSIP SPOILS MY FRIENDSHIPS'

Gossip has a bad name. People fear it when they feel that when they're not there the gossip will be against them. Or they feel uneasy at the tales friends tell, in case it's malicious or inaccurate. But gossip can be the glue that keeps social groups together. Clearly, telling spiteful stories with the aim of bringing someone down is unacceptable. But is that necessarily what gossip is about? Sometimes people gossip because they want to feel superior – in possession of knowledge other people don't have. And, if they don't have a good titbit to elevate themselves, they may make one up or exaggerate. Most times gossip is an entrance ticket – it's what you offer the other people in the group to justify your place there.

However, many times it's news and views on the people you know, with no intention of being unpleasant or unfair – and often, it passes along information that can help. It bonds the people gossiping together, but it can also alert them to a friend who needs support and something they can do to offer it.

What should you do? The key to making sure that gossip doesn't spoil a situation is always to insist that gossip be truthful and accurate, and neither judgemental nor critical.

'WE KEEP FALLING OUT'

Some friends can squabble and fight and a day later be in touch as if nothing had happened. But others find quarrels slowly or quickly lead to a bust-up that lasts.

> *'I knew this friend from schooldays and we were close. But we always seemed to argue, about nothing. And then one day we had a shouting match and I didn't call back and neither did she. I miss her but I haven't seen her for ten years.'*

Why are some friendships fractious? One reason could be that your friendship style is based on your childhood relationships. These tend to be intense and argumentative, with great closeness but equally big flare-ups. As you get older, you will change in many ways, and some of your relationships may be based on more adult patterns – just as strong but less inclined to flare and explode. It may be that those friendships you retain from your youth are still set in these more volatile patterns, or that in any friendship you revert to old habits.

What should you do? If you do find this a problem, the answer is to think about shifting your responses to a more adult mode.

We can all act as child, parent or adult in our private and working lives and on occasion. The thing is that certain situations arise where we may find ourselves falling into one of those roles without realizing it – bossing people around as the parent or misbehaving as a child when it's actually inappropriate. What often happens is that we take that role when we're with people with whom we're used to playing that role. So parents when they're with their grown-up children will act like a parent rather than an adult, and their children immediately start acting like infants again. Or two old friends, used to being kids with each other, will assume those childhood patterns even when they behaving like adults with everyone else.

Child, parent, adult

We all carry within us several ego states – parts of our personality that cause us to act in different ways in different situations:

* We can be the **child** – reacting with pure feeling, and in the ways we responded when we were young. The child wants to run in the wet grass and damn the consequences. The child sulks when its faults are pointed out.

* We can be the **parent**, reacting the way we have been taught, the way our parents taught us – doing all the things we 'ought' to do, and telling everyone else how to behave. The parent is the one doing the telling-off, who takes charge and directs.

* And we can be the **adult**, reacting in ways that we have learned work – sensible, rational and by negotiation and agreement. The adult shares responsibility and takes knock-backs as chances to do better.

When someone goes 'child' on you, it's quite hard not to go either 'child' or 'parent' on them; when someone assumes the 'parent' role, it's so easy to slip into being a child. If you find that conflict always comes in whenever you see certain people, it's worth having a think about whether the problem going on is child/parent/adult. Consciously work at being an adult and you may find that they take on that role, too, and that the arguments cease.

'I DON'T LIKE THE PARTNER'

A common reason for losing touch with a friend is when a partner comes on the scene, either theirs or yours. On the whole, if two people have a connection, anyone each of them forms a bond with should be compatible with the other. But that's not always true. And, of course, love can be blind; they may not see the flaw that a friend can spot. Possessiveness and jealousy can play a part, too. The new partner may want to make themselves the centre of their lover's life and resent old friends who have more of a history. Or you may be the one feeling jealous of being displaced and – being on the lookout for faults – easily see them.

What should you do? Examine your own responses and feelings and be honest – is the difficulty in the way you see the situation? Are you the one feeling jealous or left out? If so, perhaps you need to concentrate on your own love life – if yours is going well, you may feel better about the fact that your friend has someone important and intimate in their life. If it isn't, that may be the area in your life that needs attention. If it's simply a case of you and the partner not hitting it off, for the sake of your friend you need to be adult and be polite. If you have serious doubts about this person, then the best thing you can do is say you and they don't get on and that's fine; you'll take a back seat but will always be there for your friend. See your friend on their own and maintain the closeness – if the new partner is a 'wrong 'un', your friend will need you when the whole thing blows up. Criticizing the partner seldom helps – you'll just become the messenger that gets shot.

Key idea: 'I wish you'd told me'

When we choose a partner we invest in them, and criticism of them not only calls the person we've chosen into doubt; it also calls our abilities to discern and choose into doubt. So, naturally, we're likely to be defensive rather than to want to listen. But how often does a friend say, after a break-up: 'I wish you'd told me!' The best tactic is to say that you have a problem with the new partner and that you don't hit it off, or to point out a specific issue that has arisen, and then withdraw from socializing with them as a couple, while keeping contact with the friend.

'I'M NOT SURE WHAT TO DO – MY FRIEND IS GOING THROUGH A DIVORCE'

Friendships often fragment when a separation or a divorce happens, or a new family is formed. Even good friends can shy away when a relationship breaks down. Just when you feel at your most vulnerable and in need of supporters, friends can get cold feet. Sometimes it's because they think they have to take sides rather than face the delicate task of being still friends but neutral, and you become the one that gets dropped. More often, both ex-partners find themselves out in the cold. Separation and divorce are scary issues and superstitiously we often fear they are catching – become involved, and we too may go down that route. Often, one half of a couple fears that their partner may get ideas, or be attracted to the newly available friend.

Even if they stay the course through the break-up, friends may feel uncomfortable when a new family is established. Groups of couples especially can find it hard when John and Jane become John and Mary or Jane and Steve, or John and Steve become John and Bob.

What should you do? People often feel that it's difficult to split their allegiance, but that's what adults do. Consider the fact that you don't stop loving one child because another comes along, or your partner because you now have children to attend to. If you were friends with both halves of a couple, you can continue being so, and if a new person comes along, you simply have to take a deep breath, welcome them in and make a new friend. With the way marriage is going in the Western world, if you don't follow this line you will soon lose half your friends, and for no good reason.

'I'VE GOT DIFFERENT GROUPS OF FRIENDS – HOW CAN THEY GET ON?'

Maybe you have a small and select group of friends who all know each other and share tastes. More often we pick up friends as we go through life, from school and college, various workplaces, through shared interests... it can be endless. But it can be a pity when, as we make new friends, we drop old ones, especially if the reason is that you feel that the new ones have different outlooks and so won't get on with the old ones.

What should you do? We all have different aspects of ourselves and our friends can reflect that. You don't stop, say, being fond of going to pub quiz nights because you also take up cycling. And it's perfectly possible to manage and balance having different friends from different eras of your life or parts of your present life. Don't worry if they are disparate – they don't have to meet except at large events in your life such as weddings and anniversaries, and then it can be fun rather than stressful to see what they make of each other.

Top tips for making and keeping friends

One of the main markers for ill health and depression is whether you have friends. People with few active friendships tend to be more depressed and less healthy. And it's not good enough to know lots of people, whom you hardly ever see. You'll have fewer regrets in life, and be both healthier and happier, if you make the effort to keep your relationships strong, happy and ongoing. Ring for a chat, interact through social messaging, but most of all make the time to talk face to face. There's no substitute for spending time together and communicating.

▶ **Think and speak kind.** Spiteful gossip and smart quips about people may make you the centre of attention, but it's not going to make you any friends. It also builds up a fund of suspicion and resentment aimed at your head – and you may not think that has an effect but it does. Instead of clever malice, think kind thoughts and express them – you'll be pleasantly surprised how much it gains you in life, if only because you have no reason to feel guilty and bad.

▶ **Steer clear of making comparisons.** Measure yourself up against other people and either you feel superior – and that's not always kind or healthy – or you feel inferior – and that's definitely depressing. The best spur to improvement is to measure yourself up against yourself – to look to past performance and future goals, and to pat yourself on the back for doing your best. When it comes to other people, especially children, making comparisons between them can spread only misery and conflict. Again, encourage self-assessment and self-praise. Doing your best is the goal, not beating others.

▶ **Let it go.** Maintaining grudges and resentments are sure ways of keeping hold of regrets. By hugging bitterness to you, you keep your thoughts focused on the past rather than on the future. It's not only bad for your health – anxiety and stress can lead to depression and a range of physical conditions – it saps your energy and interferes with good relationships. Learn to take a deep breath and let it go.

▶ **Cultivate the skill of listening.** Sometimes, it's both useful and enlightening to listen – to music, to someone's ideas, to what a friend wants to tell you. It's very easy to get into the bad habit of not attending to what is being said but be simply waiting till the other person stops talking so you can say your piece. There's an art to listening, and letting the other person know you are doing so. It can transform any encounter – with a friend, a colleague, a family member – from just part of your day to a joy and perhaps a revelation.

Remember this: Points to consider

▶ Friendships are living things that develop and change. You will need to keep them healthy by paying constant care and attention to them and adjusting to meet any new shifts.

▶ As well as looking after existing friendships, keep looking for and making new connections. Friendships should be a support, not just a comfortable rut to jog along in.

▶ Learning to say 'sorry' or to apologize appropriately can be the most useful part of your servicing friendship toolbox.

▶ It's to this last point that we will turn next as part of your action plan.

Your Action Plan: Step 2 – say sorry

Step 2 of the Action Plan is saying sorry. If you have regrets and would like to dispel or reduce them, and make sure that they don't come back to haunt you later in your life, you do need to face up to them. An apology might be due to yourself and those whom you might have let down by making a choice you regret. (We'll look in the next chapter at what you do if you feel that it's someone else's responsibility.)

We so often find saying sorry hard – we cling to being right or it not really being our fault or it being more important to keep our reputation. Adults feel especially reluctant to apologize to children, as if the semblance of being in charge and infallible is more important than the actuality.

WHY SHOULD YOU APOLOGIZE?

Saying sorry to yourself allows you to move on and make better choices. Saying sorry to other people allows you to do better in future. Both help you feel better about yourself. And, if you're worried about what it looks like, consider this: people tend to know when you have been wrong and have wronged them. Even a child who has been told that adults know best will realize something is wrong. If you persist in refusing to give an apology, either a child will begin to doubt themselves, with consequent effects on their self-esteem and self-confidence, or they will resent and lose trust in you. If you have a regret about something you have done, your regret is compounded by the guilt you will feel about withholding an apology.

Key idea: Sooner rather than later...

Sooner rather than later is a good time to say sorry – later is far better than never.

HOW DO YOU SAY SORRY?

Begin by making a list of the things you'd like to apologize for and to whom. This doesn't have to be a realistic list – the people you'd like to go back and express regret to don't have to be contactable; they may even be dead. And the issues you want

to say sorry about don't need to be big, earth-shattering ones –
you may find yourself recalling things that seem trivial on paper.
That's half the point. Getting them down may help you to get
them into perspective.

Put your list in order. You may want to divide it into:

▶ things you want to say sorry to yourself about

▶ things you want to say sorry to someone else about

then into:

▶ apologies over big issues

▶ apologies over small issues

then into:

▶ apologies to people with whom I am in close contact

▶ apologies to people I'm still in contact with but who live at
a distance

▶ apologies to people I'm no longer in contact with

▶ apologies to people who are dead.

TO WHOM?

▶ Things you want to say sorry to yourself about

Regrets often fall into this category. We look back and beat
ourselves up about the wrong choices, the foolish decisions, the
things we should have or shouldn't have done. Some might be
big issues that have changed the course of your life – marrying
even though we realized the night before that this was not the
right decision, or turning down a job we really wanted because
we didn't think we could manage it. Some might be small –
saying something in public we thought made us look foolish or
losing a belonging we miss.

Whether big or large, saying sorry to yourself is a good template
to apologizing to anyone else. It can demonstrate several
important things. One is that simply putting it into words can
often help: 'I wish I'd done it differently and I'm sorry.' Another
is that you take a lesson. Whatever it was you regret, make

efforts not to do that again, and by acknowledging the situation you can make sure you change your future behaviour. Ignoring it means repeating it.

Take responsibility for your failings rather than trying to push the blame on to anyone else. If you did it, recognize that and own the problem – no excuses or fudges. Offer amends to yourself – what can you do now or in the future to make up for the past? As well as resolving not to make the same mistake, give yourself some reparation – another chance, a new opportunity. And, once you've put a sincere apology on the table, move on. Let it go. Don't worry about it again.

▶ Things you want to say sorry to someone else about

When you say sorry to someone else, keep the same rules in mind. Take responsibility. Say 'I'm sorry I...' Even if you think other people were involved or there were mitigating circumstance, this is about an apology, so give it. Just saying it makes such a difference.

Making an apology will make you feel better. However, it won't redress the situation if that is your only motive for saying sorry. Sometimes it's really important to ask yourself why you want to make this confession. To clear the air? To reveal a secret? Regrets can be like a nasty parcel that leaks dirty oil all over your life. Hug it to you and it soils everything, which is probably why you want to discard it. And if you've hurt someone and they too have part ownership of the parcel, they will thank you if you put it on the table, unwrap it and then, together with them, throw it away.

Sometimes, however, people say sorry simply to dump the parcel in the other person's lap. That might make you feel better but it leaves them holding the whole horrible mess. You have the responsibility of making sure that both of you can come out of it in a better state. That might mean you have to deal with your disclosure in a different way. It might mean involving a professional – a mediator or a counsellor – on your own or with the other person. And it may mean dealing with the regret on your own, if disclosing it is only going to hurt the other person to no good end.

Key idea: Who benefits?

Always ask yourself, and always answer honestly: 'Who will benefit from this apology?'

OVER WHAT?

▶ **Big issues**

Most regrets are about big issues. They can be about always putting work before family and never having time for your children. Or taking the easy option instead of going for broke when it came to choosing exams to take or a course or a job to apply for. Or starting, or continuing, an argument that has meant you've feuded with someone for years. They can be about issues that sent you down one road in your life so that, looking back, you think: 'Things would have been so different if only…' You may then feel that going back and apologizing would be futile. Something that significant can't be changed, so what's the point of trying, even though you frequently, if not on a daily basis, regret what happened?

Of course, you are right that you can't regress and change the past. But you'd be surprised at the power that making a stand and making a change even at a very late date can have. Recognizing the significance of a past mistake, accepting responsibility for your own part in it, saying sorry to yourself or other people, can all trigger relief. If you can let go of past defensiveness, anger, resentment and arrogance, you'll be amazed at how much better you can feel – at how much pain you can heal and how much joy you can bring to others.

Most important of all, tackling the big regrets, even though started or grounded in the past, and even though you may feel it's too late to do anything about them, can lead to significant changes.

We're often scared to apologize for three reasons:

1 **We think the other person will reject the apology.** This is the worst-case scenario, and yet, even if they do, we'll still have the satisfaction and relief of having made the attempt. In reality, while many people might be nonplussed at first and still so angry they could hesitate, most apologies are received in the spirit in which they are given, and do lead to a reconciliation.

2 **We think the other person will gain power over us and that we will lose authority.** There's nothing weak in acknowledging that you have made a mistake. Having the strength to acknowledge a mistake or a wrongdoing gives you moral authority. And it allows the other person to recover their pride, something that you may owe them.

3 **You believe it won't make a difference.** It may. And not trying certainly leaves you stuck in the same situation. So why not try?

Even issues such as letting go of dreams and ambitions can and should be tackled.

Case study: Carla

Carla had always had a bad relationship with her younger sister, Julia, since they were small. Carla was three years older and had been furious to have a baby foisted – as she saw it –upon her. They rowed all through childhood and their teens and avoided each other after Carla went to university. When they saw each other over Christmas holidays at their parents' they were frostily polite. They finally had a massive quarrel at Julia's wedding, when Carla brought the boy she eventually married but whom Julia said hadn't been invited. From then on they visited their parents only when the other was not there, and when they could not avoid being in the same place, such as at weddings and funerals, maintained a distance.

As both got older, Carla deeply regretted falling out and kept wondering whether she should get in touch, but always backed off, feeling that Julia would only reject any approach. Anyway, wasn't it now too late? On her 70th birthday, Carla rang her sister and poured out a prepared speech about how sorry she was they had avoided each other and how much she wished they could be friends. After a lengthy silence, Julia said she felt the same and maybe they should meet. Unknown to Carla, Julia had cancer. They reconciled and found that they had so much in common and now really liked each other. Julia died eight months later and while grieving for the loss of her sister and the waste of more than 40 years, Carla could at least rejoice in the past months of closeness.

Case study: Geoff

Geoff always wanted to play the piano seriously, possibly even
professionally. He'd been encouraged by one teacher at his school but,
although his parents bought him an old upright piano to practise on,
they discouraged any idea of making this a career and pressured him into
taking a course in engineering, not music. He still played, but when he
married his wife said she hated the noise and he eventually let her sell
the piano. It remained a point of contention between them, and when
he retired he finally snapped, told her he now had time to do what he
really wanted and, if she didn't like it, she could go and stay with her
sister. He bought a grand piano, installed it in the main room, found a
music tutor and played. He was surprised to find that, in spite of his age
and the length of time he had not played, he still had skills, and improved
enormously over the next few years. His children and grandchildren loved
it and were most impressed. His wife... well, she got used to it.

▶ Small issues

It's easy to see how going back to address a big issue may be
important, if hard. But what about the small niggles – the
regrets over losing a toy, rejecting an invitation, being too shy
to accept a compliment? You need to address these, too, and
for two main reasons. One is that small niggles add up. You
regret this, you regret that, and if you trace them you begin to
realize that your big problem is that you spend too much time
looking backwards having regrets! But when you do examine
them you may find that a small regret actually masks a big
one. As a teenager, you refused compliments, you didn't accept
an invitation, you avoided someone you actually liked. But as
an adult you also kept your head down and tried to be in the
background. Your real problem is one of poor self-esteem and
self-confidence and, once you recognize it, there's certainly
something you can, and should, do about it.

THE LEVEL OF CONTACT

▶ Apologies to people you are in close contact with

You may decide to begin your apologies to the people you see
most often, who are close to you – your partner, family and

children. In some cases the trust you have between you can make these approaches the most comfortable, and so a good way of easing yourself into the task. But sometimes it can make it hardest. 'Love means never having to say you're sorry' is sadly a well-known phrase – perhaps one of the stupidest and most pernicious bits of nonsense ever to have come out of Hollywood! Saying sorry is part of a good relationship and of love. You should never assume the people closest to you know what you really meant and can forgive you your mistakes – you have to *say* it.

How to apologize?

Apologies are best done face to face. Failing that, use electronic media of a kind that at least gets you as close as possible to that experience – a video call or voice call. If that's not possible, a handwritten letter is better than an email or text message, though even those are better than nothing. Making your apology public on social media would quite rightly call into question your motives for doing it. Are you asking for applause, or making a private communication?

Here are a few basic guidelines for making an apology:

* **Think about your body language and your tone of voice**. You show real regret and a wish to make amends by the way you lean forward, make eye contact and use a warm tone.
* **Think about your words**. Take responsibility for what happened, even if other people were also involved. Use 'I' statements – 'I feel', 'I think', 'I would like' – so that you own what you are saying, rather than 'you' statements, which shift responsibility on to others.
* **Set your mind on making amends** and coming away from this encounter with both of you feeling better. You can explain yourself but avoid trying to excuse, justify or defend yourself.
* **Make no assumptions** about what the other person might be or was feeling or thinking, but be open to hearing them out when you have said your piece. You might not like what you hear because they may want to vent or express anger or disappointment at the past. But if you hold to the line of wanting to make a difference, they too are likely to come over to seeing this as an opportunity to improve the situation. Similarly, make no demands – you can't put conditions or ultimatums on saying sorry. If you do, the apology is neither sincere nor honest, and is likely to trigger further upset, not reconciliation.

* **Remember the acronym KISS – Keep It Simple, Stupid**. Avoid long explanations. Just the facts, ma'am.
* **Offer amends**. This may simply be the apology itself, but you might want of think of something you can do, for yourself if the apology is to yourself, or for the other person or people. It can be in the form of restitution or by making it clear how you intend to behave in the future to ensure that this does not happen again.
* **Take the lesson**. My old mum used to say, 'Don't say sorry – just don't do it again!' Well, I say: 'Do say sorry and don't do it again.' Often, we repeat mistakes because we don't want to acknowledge that we have failed or got something wrong. If you don't want to hurt yourself or other people any more, the best thing is to recognize and acknowledge failure and learn from it.
* **Forgive yourself**. Being forgiven by someone we've offended is lovely, and the fear that they won't take our apology is often what holds us back. But having taken the step, whether they do (most likely) or don't (rarely) accept your apology, if it was sincerely and honestly offered, give yourself a pat on the back and let go your feelings of remorse and move on.

Key idea

Love – and friendship – mean *always* having to say you're sorry.

▶ Apologies to people you're still in contact with but who live at a distance

All the strategies above stand with one difference, which is that your apology may have to be other than face to face. If it's important, you might think it worth it to make a journey. Making such an effort would certainly hammer home the point that you are sincere. But a carefully worded and beautifully written letter would start the ball rolling, making your intentions clear.

▶ Apologies to people you're no longer in contact with

You can often get back in touch with people from your past through those you have kept contact with – old friends, family members, people from your old haunts. The development in social media also makes it possible to find old friends and family members with whom you have no connection. Using all the skills already outlined, you can approach them – but note the caution about using the public areas of social media. If you don't have an address or phone number, a written note is fine even if it is through email or message. A full-on apology for sins past is not advisable on someone's Facebook page or Twitter feed. As already said, are you looking for applause or a genuine reconciliation?

▶ **Apologies to people who are dead**

But what if you wished you could say something to someone you can't find, or who you know is dead? Does that have to mean your apology cannot be delivered and your regret has to continue? The answer is no – and we're not talking séances here, either. While one important aspect of an apology to address a regret is making it to the person involved, the other half – well, actually, more than half – is the effect it has on you. Considering the regret, addressing the situation that led to it, exploring the ramifications and resolving to offer an apology are all profound, and often life-changing, actions. You won't go back from it, and although you will feel sad that it is not possible to know what the other person's reaction would be, you still benefit. Similarly, if all you can do is mull over what you would like to have said, that in itself is helpful. If you want to say something important to someone who is beyond your reach, this is what you do.

Try it now: Send an apology to somebody out of reach

1 Write your message – as long as you like, as involved as you like. Put the situation down on paper and say what you'd have liked to have done to redress it and what you intend doing in the future.
2 Then, alone or with trusted family or friends, set up a time and place where you can burn the letter – in a fireplace, on a bonfire, in a barbeque or simply in an ashtray on the front step or in the park.
3 Gather round, raise a toast to the absent person and send them your message on the wings of flames and smoke. As the letter is reduced to ashes, know your message has gone to them, and you can let it go.

'At the end of your life, you will never regret not having passed one more test, not winning one more verdict or not closing one more deal. You will regret time not spent with a husband, a friend, a child, or a parent.'

Barbara Bush

Focus points

✳ Nobody can do it on their own – we all need a support network to help us get by.

✳ Whether your support is from family or friends, it should be reciprocal and paid for by returning the favour.

✳ Friends will not beat a path to your door – they have to be looked for and earned.

✳ Maintaining friendships is all-important – they can fade or die if not cared for regularly.

✳ The Internet is still only 20 years old and it requires new codes of behaviour and new rules. Making online friends may seem quick and easy, but be aware of the drawbacks and take care.

✳ Friends are only human and therefore never perfect. They can change, make mistakes and have misunderstandings. Patience, toleration and adjustment will all be needed.

✳ All your friends do not have to be compatible. Don't drop a particular one just because they don't fit in with the rest.

✳ Friendships can break up over misunderstandings or what is seen as offence. Being able to say 'sorry' or to apologize where it is appropriate is the way to avoid this.

✳ Learn how to forgive yourself.

✳ Saying 'sorry' for a past offence, particularly if it was against somebody who is now out of reach, can give you a marvellous emotional release.

Next step

The next chapter, on dreams and ambitions, looks at how these might be frustrated – leading to later regret – and how to use your Action Plan to deal with past, present and future regrets.

4

'I wish I had pursued my dreams and ambitions'

In this chapter you will learn:

▶ *How early ambitions can become frustrated and lead to the beginning of regrets*

▶ *How to become a 'better late than never' life-changer*

▶ *How to use your Action Plan to deal with regrets of the past, present or future.*

'When I grow up...'

Sometime in your life you wanted to be a train driver or a
nurse, a model or an astronaut. You might have wanted to be
a movie star, a singer or an artist, or to write books or songs
or plays. You might have imagined yourself as prime minister
or president, or the best in the world at whatever it is you love
doing. And you wanted to travel, to marry someone fabulous,
to be surrounded by acclaim and attention. Some people hold
on to their dreams and make them work. Many of us 'get real'
and look back on those ambitions with derision or sadness,
envying the people who did make it and wondering what it was
that set us on a different route. Those regrets may not just be
about grandiose ambitions that bit the dust, but realistic wishes
that somehow got left behind. Several of the respondents to my
questionnaire regretted never having learned languages such as
German, French or Spanish, or dropping out of learning to play
musical instruments, to skate or to swim.

Settling for second best

There are so many reasons why we tend to settle for second
best. Maybe we were told our aspirations were unrealistic or
that we didn't have the abilities to achieve them. One of the
respondents to my questionnaire said:

> 'I regret not having enough confidence in myself at a young
> age – i.e. not considered very intelligent/bright by others
> has an effect on decisions you make or how you do things.'

Sometimes we feel that our responsibilities to others have meant
that we had to aim lower. Simon said:

> 'I had a place at university but then my father died. In all
> the chaos after, I never went but got a job to look after
> my mother and sisters. The stupid thing was that when
> we finally talked it over several years later, when both my
> sisters had gone to university, my mother was distraught
> I'd made that decision. She said she'd never have asked me
> to do it or wanted me to do so – she was just overwhelmed
> and, when she did wake up to the fact I hadn't gone, she
> thought I'd made it as a real choice.'

Perhaps we paid attention to what other people said without thinking through what their motives, reasons or needs might be. One respondent said:

'I regret allowing myself to be influenced by the wrong people, parents, peers, things I read. Not trying to think things out for myself, believing other people knew better and that I should pay attention to their beliefs and opinions.'

Another said:

'I regret giving in to someone else's opinion about my university selection. Someone else at school wanted to apply for one of my options and my school said only one person should apply to each college so I went for another and didn't like my time there. She didn't get in to the college she'd picked, but another of my good friends did go there and had an amazing time. I wish I'd had the courage not to have given in – maybe I'd have had a better time at university if I had.'

Family finances, family expectations and a host of issues could result in our veering off on a different path from the one we'd imagined or hoped for. Or perhaps we tried and fell at the first hurdle, or someway down the path, and retreated, bruised and battered, accepting that it just wasn't going to happen. Well-meaning parents, teachers and carers can often put us off – rather than have us suffer the pain of failure they may discourage us by reassuring us that we don't need to make another stab at it. Or perhaps we may have been protected from failure in the first place by never being allowed to compete and strive. Giving everyone at a school sports day a medal may mean that nobody feels bad at the time, but it also means that nobody learns how to overcome disappointment by having to work hard the next time.

Whatever the reason, so many of us are left with simmering resentment about the things we wanted to achieve, the places we wanted to go, and didn't: 'I wish I'd learned languages', 'I wish I'd gone to acting school', 'I wish I'd gone round the world' are frequent plaints.

Is it too late to change?

Is it always too late? You'd think so, because most of us accept that after a certain age we can't go back to learning or take risks with our livelihood. And we feel that we're set in our ways, that ambition and endeavour belong to the young. Yet, looking around us, we can find plenty of examples of people who have jumped tracks and not only tried but succeeded in a new and often exceptionally ambitious field at an age that most of us feel would be far too late to begin a new career.

Late starters

* **Andrea Bocelli** didn't start singing opera seriously until the age of 34.
* **Alan Rickman** and **Danny Glover** didn't begin acting until they were 28 and Rickman's first big and successful movie role was at the age of 46.
* **Stan Lee**, creator of Spider-Man, was 43 when he began drawing his legendary superheroes.
* **Julia Child**, who worked for the government as a spy, didn't start teaching cooking until she was nearly 40. She first went to cookery school at 36.
* **Leonard Cohen** released his first album when he was 33 years old.
* **Richard Adams**, author of the bestselling *Watership Down*, didn't get his novel published until he was in his fifties.
* **Flora Thompson** achieved writing fame with *Lark Rise to Candleford* at the age of 63, **Kenneth Grahame** published *Wind in the Willows* in his retirement.
* **Raymond Chandler** published his first short story at 45 and his first novel, *The Big Sleep*, at 51.
* Actor **Brain Blessed** made the first of three attempts to climb Everest in his fifties.
* Folk artist **'Grandma Moses'** became a painter in her seventies.
* **Harland Sanders** tried his hand at being a steamboat pilot, an insurance salesman, a farmer and a fireman and then ran a service station where he cooked chicken for passing motorists. When the station closed because the new interstate reduced traffic, he retired and spent his first social security cheque on setting his chicken restaurants up as a franchise... which became KFC.

And those are just the celebrities. What about the examples you might be able to find in your own backyard of people who have gone back and started again, often reviving long-held ambitions and realizing them, or at least gaining enormous satisfaction by trying to do so? I know someone, a doctor and psychoanalyst, who gained a law degree at the age of 82. Two of her siblings and her father had been lawyers – how satisfying to go one better and have both degrees. Using new technology and opportunities, several people I know have realized long-cherished ambitions to publish books. These may not become bestsellers but they are freely available on the Internet and their authors have the immense achievement of being able to hold a copy of their dreams in their hands. Another friend fulfilled his ambition of cycling round the coast of Scotland – every little inlet and shoreline – just before his 60th birthday.

THE FUTURE CAN BE CHANGED

It is true that you cannot go back and change the past, but there are several differences nowadays in comparison to the past that can significantly affect your ability to change your future and rectify a regret. One is that we are living longer and in better health. Previous generations may have had to accept that with some ambitions you're simply not up to it once you've passed a certain age. Who ever heard of so many professions or jobs or even pastimes being anything but the preserve of the young? Well – now, we do. When some of our iconic pop stars are in their late sixties and early seventies (Mick Jagger, 69; Keith Richards, 69; Tina Turner, 73), our lusted-after film stars in their fifties and sixties (George Clooney, 52; Christine Baranski, 60), our admired fashion models in their forties (Naomi Campbell, 43; Cameron Alborzian, 46), it's no longer good enough to insist that our day has gone.

Another is that, with longer and healthier lives and changes in the way we run our working lives, we no longer assume we'll have a job for life. If it's often necessary to shift not only from one job to another but from one career to another, it's also now taken for granted that we often have to learn new skills and ideas. Training and education are open to all ages, so it's eminently possible to begin again, whatever stage in life you are at.

BARRIERS TO CHANGE

Finances may be a barrier to be overcome but the greatest barrier could be your own reticence – perhaps arising from a fear of what other people might think. Am I too old? Is it too late? Am I being silly to want to do this? Will people feel I'm trespassing on territory better left to the young, or even that I'm cheating by trying to do it now? As well as a fear of being laughed at or thought unrealistic, sometimes people feel that if they take action late in life it's as if you're acknowledging and accepting you could have done it sooner, and that would suggest you wasted your opportunities.

Case study: Wayne

Wayne avoided facing up to his claustrophobia for years. He said: 'Even though she didn't complain, I knew it hurt my wife, who would have liked to have taken holidays involving flights. As it is, we could go no further than what we could reach by car and ferry or train.' When it came to a head and caused bitter rows, Wayne finally accepted her suggestion to see a counsellor. He found himself saying that, if he did get treatment and it worked, he'd blame himself even more for having left it so long.

While his refusal to fly stayed as it was, it was as if it couldn't be helped and was not his fault. Wayne was helped to see that, if he continued to stay as he was, the waste would not be of the past, because he couldn't help that. The true waste would be if he didn't act now, knowing that he could change the future. He came round to accepting that it was never too late and that he could act, to make a difference now and for the future. Even a few years, a few months or days, of enjoying something you've deprived yourself of for years is better than no years, no months, no days, he decided.

And, as he said, the chances are that, once you do make changes, it's going to be a lot more than that and will leave a legacy. His children had spent all their childhood accepting that Dad didn't fly. They did go on holidays abroad with their school and with their friends and grandparents, but had said that they were sad they'd never shared those adventures with him. But their first family trip to a villa holiday in Italy with Wayne and their mother, Trudy, with their own partners and children, was pronounced by the whole family as being the best they had ever had and something they would all never forget. 'Better late than never' was the general feeling.

Remember this: Points to consider

▶ Have your early ambitions faded and has your life become one of accepting second best?

▶ What might have been is one of the most common causes of regret.

▶ It's never too late and you can change your future.

▶ The examples of others who did make a change can inspire you – and you could in turn inspire others!

Fulfilling your dreams and inspiring others

Some dreams and ambitions can be followed late. It may not be the same as if you had done it first time around, but in fact there is an argument that you might not have got as much out of some things when young as you would when older, more mature, more thoughtful and maybe more skilled. And certainly you might get more satisfaction out of it, knowing the effort that has gone into succeeding. Anya said:

> 'I always, always had this silly ambition to run a marathon. I knew I couldn't do it and my ex-husband kept telling me so, so I never did. Then we divorced and some friends persuaded me to do it, as a way of cocking a snook at him and celebrating my 50th. I did it. And I did it in 4 hours 59 minutes and 59 seconds. I broke 5 hours!! OK, the world record for a woman is 2 hours 15, but for me that was an achievement I couldn't even dream about. I can't tell you how good I felt, and how much it's helped me do other things I wanted to do – such as retraining for a great new job!'

As for Anya, finding hidden and abandoned ambitions, unlocking stifled talents, gaining new skills and researching opportunities can do far more than simply settling a long-awaited or forgotten aspiration. It can springboard you into new opportunities that you might not otherwise have considered.

Some 30 years ago I went on an Outward Bound course, which included climbing and abseiling. As someone acutely afraid of heights, I found these pursuits terrifying but I had wanted to do them from my schooldays. I faced my fears and achieved an ambition, and came back home to decide to leave a secure job, move to the Lake District and take up a career as a full-time freelance writer. Becoming a counsellor, an agony aunt, a parenting educator, a charity trustee and a writer all sprang from the moment I stood at the top of a cliff and ventured over it on the end of a rope. Several of the people I worked with at the time thought I was being ridiculous to waste my time and money on that holiday. I can confidently say to anyone wondering whether to ask themselves 'What's my lost ambition or dream and should I try to realize it?' that it's more likely to be a gain than a loss if you do.

Of course, you may have to scale back your ambition or do it in a different way. The challenge may lie in considering what you could do in the spirit of the past desire, rather than simply giving up and consigning it to the dustbin of history. Stewart said:

> 'I'd wanted to climb Everest when I was young and my father poured cold water on any such ambition. I'm a dad myself now and I'd never, ever tell my children their dreams are rubbish. And five years ago I took a pay cut to be able to come and live in the Lake District so that I can climb and walk in the Fells as often as possible. I may never be a somebody in the mountaineering world, but I get to do something I love with my family and friends, and that's more than good enough for me.'

One element of going back and addressing a lost dream or ambition is the help it might give other people as well as yourself. What Stewart has found is the impetus to listen to and support his children's dreams, because he wasn't encouraged to pursue his own. And his example, finding a scaled-back but satisfying version of what he had wanted to do, is also an inspiration to them. His example told them that it was good to go for your dreams, that it was never too late, and that, if necessary, you could adjust and be realistic in order to achieve them. But he emphasized that although, all things considered, he was happy to enjoy what he had, they should never assume it was right to be less than determined.

'I've never travelled'

One frequent regret, voiced by many of my respondents, is that they never travelled as much as they might have liked. 'We've taken holidays abroad, of course, but never off the beaten track as I've always wanted to do,' said one. 'I'd fantasized about hitching to Istanbul when I was a student but when it came to it, the whole thing just terrified me. I've always wished I'd done it.' The simple answer is – why not? OK – maybe you no longer feel able to hitch and the discomfort of sleeping rough would be unpleasant rather than an adventure, but why not use cheap flights or trains or your car to take you to new and less visited places as a couple or a family? And why does it need to be out-of-the way places to give you a glimpse of other lives, other places? A series of quick city breaks, taken on the spur of the moment, can be affordable and doable, and may satisfy that longed-for ambition. The Internet gives you the chance to research and modern transport can take you just about anywhere to begin your odyssey – all that really holds you back is fear or the myth that you've missed the boat and it's too late. *It's never too late.*

Remember this: Points to consider

- Dealing with your regrets means examining honestly what really caused them.

- Following the strategies in the Action Plan can be your best path to reducing or removing your regrets.

- Be ambitious and aim high. Then, even a partial achievement will give you some satisfaction and less to regret.

- Make positive choices and be responsible for them. Regrets are then less likely to happen.

Your Action Plan: Step 3 – confront and accept what has led to your regrets

So we're at step 3 of your Action Plan. Having identified what it is you regret and said sorry to yourself and anyone else you might have harmed or offended, it now helps to confront and accept what it was that led to your regrets.

Exploring what surrounded the circumstances of your feelings of loss and sadness may mean pointing a finger. You may find yourself saying 'I did it because of this or that … or so-and-so.' Abi, for instance, says:

> 'I know exactly why I lost out on something I've always wanted. I was 11 years old and wanted more than anything else to be in a rock band. My granddad bought me a guitar and I spent every minute I had learning to play that sucker. When I failed one test at school, my teacher found out from my parents what I did in my spare time and he made it his business to come down on me. Every time I saw him he'd go on and on about what an idiot I was and how talentless and stupid, until just to shut him up I gave my guitar away. It shouldn't have but it really got to me.'

Abi went to university and has a good career as an accountant. But, he says:

> 'I don't think I ever felt as happy as on my 50th birthday when my fabulous, darling, perceptive wife gave me a guitar and a series of lessons with a local session musician. I now play in a band. Nothing earth-shattering – we do weddings and local stuff. And, of course, it's not the same as it might have been. But hey – it's like healing a wound I've had all these years. And sometimes I think of that sadistic bastard and imagine I'm playing a riff on his grave!'

Sometimes being able to recognize the voice that told you that you couldn't do something allows you to shrug off the influence it might still have. One exercise I recommend is burying the parcel.

Try it now: Burying the parcel

Think about your regret. Think about who or what told you and maybe still tells you 'No' or 'You can't' or 'You ought not' or 'You should not'.

Isolate the voice and imagine it's coming from a parcel you are holding – a parcel that is leaking nasty, dirty oil all over your hands. The owner of the voice has given you that parcel and it's been tainting you ever since. But the reality is that you don't have to go on holding it. They, not you, chose to tell you those awful things. They, not you, own the parcel. You can do one of three things.

1 You can give it back, saying: 'This is yours and I don't want it. I don't need to go on holding it.'
2 You can throw it away, and go wash your hands.
3 You can give it to someone to hold for you, and leave it behind.

Giving the parcel back

Giving it back may involve challenging the person who caused you to let go your dreams and ambitions. Faisal wanted to act and came up against pressure from his father who opposed his career choice and said that, while he would support him going to university, he would not pay for him to go to acting school. Faisal got his degree, began work... and then, having raised enough to support himself, auditioned for and got a place in a prestigious school of drama.

When he landed his first big role in a television series, he visited his parents, who were delighted and boasted to all their friends about their son the star. But Faisal took his father aside and, having said he loved him and respected him, said he needed to tell him how angry he was at the way he nearly blocked the way to his ambitions. Faisal's father blustered at first, but Faisal felt so much better at having got it off his chest, and his confidence meant that eventually his father backed down and apologized.

Throwing the parcel away

Throwing it away means settling your own mind on the fact that this mess is none of your doing and that it's something that you no longer want to carry around. It means metaphorically washing your hands of the influence it had – and sometimes you do that best by *literally* washing your hands. Holding a private ritual by yourself, or with people you trust, you can put the issue into words then ceremonially wash it off yourself, while declaring that you are now free of it.

Katrina hated public speaking and, whenever she had to get up in front of other people, would remember her ordeals at school, being told she was useless because she hadn't done her homework when she had – she was just tongue-tied. When a promotion meant she had to give seminars, Katarina accepted her firm's offer of training, but the trainer also suggested she see a counsellor about her anxieties. One of the strategies she suggested was a 'letting go' ritual with her family that involved writing a letter and burning it, and washing her hands of her past fears. Katarina thought it was a silly idea, but she tried it and was amazed at how much better she felt afterwards and continued to feel. Her seminars are now rated as first class.

Giving the parcel to someone to hold

Giving it to someone to hold for you can involve, as it did for Katarina, seeing a counsellor and talking over whatever it is that bothers you. Unburdening yourself to a professional has the effect of 'passing the parcel'. Having talked it over, you can walk away feeling as if you have left the issue in their hands, to dispose of for you. Katarina carried out what felt like an exorcism by doing her own 'letting go' ritual, but the process was begun by seeing someone about it – and in many cases that is enough.

Being able to place where the causes of your regrets came from can help. It allows you to identify the external voice that you may have internalized. Bryony said:

> *'I really did think I was stupid and dull. I always told myself so and it meant I hung back and never tried to better myself. When my doctor sent me to talk to someone about my anxiety, she helped me realize that the voice I was hearing, if you like, was my father's. He was a cold, controlling man who left us when I was ten, but the damage had been done. Except we were able to undo it, by helping me see that I could ignore that voice, the voice of someone who didn't know me. At all. I'm a teacher now. I make sure I never, ever tell a child they are stupid – even when they are driving me to distraction!'*

Knowing your regret came from an outside influence, you can set it aside and move on. Consider:

- What did I want to do?
- Why didn't I do it?
- What can I do now or in the near future to address this in some way?

Ideas-storm with your family, friends or people you trust and come up with some ideas (see Chapter 2).

However, while it may have been someone else's initial responsibility, it would have been your responsibility if you later continued to ignore your dreams and ambitions. Placing blame only helps if it does give you the impetus to move on. It tends to make you stick in denial and anger if what you do is conclude that it was someone else's fault and that that is your free ticket to go on avoiding the issue and complaining. The key is accepting that your loss of opportunity happened and that it's now down to you to do something about it. How can you make changes?

> 'Oh, it's delightful to have ambitions. I'm so glad I have such a lot. And there never seems to be any end to them – that's the best of it. Just as soon as you attain to one ambition you see another one glittering higher up still. It does make life so interesting.'
>
> L.M. Montgomery, *Anne of Green Gables*

Top tips to help you make up for lost time

- **Allow yourself to be ambitious.** If you aim high, you can be perfectly happy to accept half of what you imagined. If you aim low, you're stuck down there. Dream ambitiously, and the chances are you'll achieve more than you had expected... and have less to regret.

- **Make choices.** Once you recognize that doing nothing is actually a choice, it becomes easier to push yourself to be active rather than passive. But will you then regret the choices you have made, thinking that things that just happened to you were at least not your responsibility? Probably not, because feeling in control of your life gives you more resilience and coping skills.

▶ **Own what you say and what you do.** Passing the buck and making excuses – 'it wasn't my fault' / 'I can't help it' – never helps. You're more likely to be in control if your attitude is to own what you say and do, and take responsibility for your words and actions.

'I'd rather be partly great than entirely useless.'
Neal Shusterman, *Unwind*

Focus points

* Many of us have frustrated early ambitions and can find ourselves living a life of second best.
* What might have been is one of the major causes of later regrets.
* There can be a choice even if it's only a partial one, to lose our regrets by making a conscious change to our lives.
* If you still need a final push to do something, it's worth getting inspiration by examining the stories of those who have made a change.
* 'Better late than never' is as good a motto as any for those who do want to achieve real change.
* You cannot move on until you have fully examined and accepted the true reasons for why you are where you are.
* You might need to use step 3 of the Action Plan to deal with the past before you can reach successfully for a new future.
* Always aim high in any enterprise. Partial success in a lofty ambition will be more rewarding than total success in a tiny one.
* Make clear, firm choices and own them. No excuses tends to mean no regrets.
* Nothing is totally set in stone. You can make changes, and even small ones will reduce your regret burden.

Next step

The next chapter is about the importance of good communication, how to improve your communication skills and how the lack of them can lead to regret.

5

'I wish I'd spoken up'

In this chapter you will learn:

▶ *About the need for communication and how the lack of it can cause regrets*

▶ *How to improve your communication skills*

▶ *How to use a self-assessment exercise to find out whether you really communicate*

▶ *How to deal with your relationships – past, present and future.*

Communication – or the lack of it!

A common regret that so many of us have revolves around communication – or lack of it. So often we fail to speak out, whether it's to object to something that is hurting or harming us, or to thank or praise or express affection. Several respondents to my questionnaire found this was something they regretted. One of them said:

> 'I regret many things left unsaid – both about how I felt and what I think in different situations. I regret not speaking out when noticing something is off just because I didn't trust my own judgement.'

Another commented:

> 'I regret not respecting myself enough to tell people how I feel about the things they did to me or said about me.'

And one more said:

> 'I regret not being more emotionally honest with a man I used to know. I might still know him now if I had.'

So many people look back and wish they'd told the people they love about their feelings – partners, children and even cherished friends, who might never have realized how valued they were because they'd never said anything. Rob said:

> 'My father was such a stern, almost forbidding figure. But I adored him and looked up to him, even though he rather baffled me by his standoffishness. Friends' fathers would hug and even kiss their sons, but I know my dad would never have any truck with that sort of thing. So when I went away after university to volunteer abroad for a year, we just sort of said 'See you' and that was that. It was the last time I saw him – he had a heart attack and died before I could get home. And my mum said that when he was in hospital he said his greatest regret was not telling me he loved me. My own sons joke about how often their sloppy dad kisses and hugs them but I think they know it's a better way.'

And one reader who wrote to me was mourning a good friend who had died unexpectedly:

> 'We were friends for 20 years but I don't think I ever told her how much she meant to me and now I never will.'

Key idea: Suffering in silence

We don't tell people how we feel about them because of embarrassment, or fear of being made vulnerable, or fear of rejection if they don't feel the same. However, anxiety over being hurt usually leads to exactly the situation you fear or, even worse, to your loved ones suffering in silence, convinced you don't really care.

Case study: Tariq

Tariq wrote to me because he was convinced that his neighbour was prejudiced and might even be nurturing a feud against him. When Tariq and his family moved into their new house he'd smile and wave at the man across the street, and the man would cut him dead. His wife would wave back and greet Tariq and his children, but her husband would stare stonily away. He became more and more anxious about this and eventually wrote to my agony column about what he could do. I pointed out that, although this man might have a problem with him, it could just as easily be that he was short-sighted or had things on his mind – two common reasons why people appear to be antagonistic but actually aren't. I suggested that Tariq actually go up to him and say hello and see what happened. Two weeks later I got a letter from Tariq to say he had done as I suggested: 'And when I got right up close to him this man gave me the biggest, friendliest smile and we chattered away for half an hour. I said to his wife I'd been talking with him and she said: "Oh, I'm so glad. He hates people knowing he's almost blind, so he often doesn't get the chance to talk to people because he never sees them coming." So you were right and that taught me – thanks!'

Don't make assumptions

We assume our partners and children know we love them – we do so much for them, isn't that enough to show that we do? And we think people will know when we are upset or hurt or feeling rejected and slighted – because don't we show it in our actions? So we don't tell them how we feel, expecting them to 'just know'. And when someone appears to ignore us or does something that distresses us, we assume it was a deliberate snub and don't pursue an explanation. The reality is that people aren't mind-readers – even people really close to each other. Often, apparently deliberately hurtful acts by other people are nothing to do with you – they were having a bad time or you misinterpreted what they said or did. We need to get into the habit of saying how we feel, and checking out with other people how *they* are feeling, too.

Not expressing our feelings

Equally, we can remain mired in anger and bitterness because we don't express our feelings of anger or resentment or seek to resolve them. The fear can be that challenging someone with whom you have had a disagreement can lead to confrontations, arguments and alienation, when the truth is that lack of communication means that such feelings increase. Deathbed reconciliations might be the stuff of good fiction but in reality they seldom work. Talking it out as soon as you realize you have a problem is so much better. And while sooner may be better than later, you can go back and address old arguments far later than you might realize. As an agony aunt and counsellor, I hear from many people that they regret not addressing an old grievance before it was too late. One man said:

'I had a bust-up with my brother – I don't even remember what it was about – and we didn't speak for 20 years. I was getting round to telling him I wished we could be mates again when he died. I can't tell you how much I regret I hadn't spoken up earlier!'

In contrast, another woman told me about the time she wrote to an old teacher of hers:

'I read an article about her and she said she was having a really hard time in her life about the time she would have been teaching me. It took me ages but I finally wrote to her telling her how much she had meant to me, how much

she had helped me and that in the midst of her distress she had made my life so much better. I got back such a lovely thank-you from her. And she died two months later. I went cold at the thought that, if I hadn't written, how much I would have regretted it.'

Communication skills and taking risks

So how can we improve communication skills and learn how to take risks so that we can have more honest, authentic relationships? How can we express our emotions and become closer to those we love, so we can settle the issues we might have? How might we learn to resolve conflicts, so we don't carry them over late into our lives, or, indeed, carry them to our graves?

THE ART OF LISTENING

One strategy to learn is the art of listening. Before you can talk, you need to listen. And communication is always two way – to do it successfully, you have to listen as well as talk.

There are three main techniques for effective and helpful listening. These are:

1 active listening

2 reflective listening

3 open questions.

Let's look at each of these in turn.

ACTIVE LISTENING

In the first two techniques the key is keeping quiet ourselves while encouraging the other person to feel able to talk to us. With active listening, we use body language to make it clear our focus and attention is on the other person. We use eye contact; we turn to towards them, and even crouch down if necessary to be on the same level. We give them our full attention, not half an eye and ear while doing something else. We avoid crossing our arms or even our legs – crossing arms particularly gives the impression that we're closed off or protected from the other person. As the person speaks we don't interrupt, but with ums and ahs and uh-huhs and nods we make it clear that we are listening and want them to go on.

REFLECTIVE LISTENING

With reflective listening we go one step further. The body language is the same and the 'no interruption' rule remains. But now we check out that we've understood by repeating back what they've said to us: 'So you're saying...' or 'Am I right in thinking you mean...?' With young children struggling to use words or string sentences together, we'd simply say their words back to them. We shouldn't, of course, laugh or make fun of their attempts and should be patient as they make their efforts.

Try it now: Practise your listening skills

You can quickly discover the power of using active and reflective listening with your partner or other family member or a friend or colleague.

1 Toss a coin for who goes first.
2 The one going first has two minutes – time it on a watch or clock or egg-timer. They can speak for that time without interruptions while the other uses active listening to encourage them on – making eye contact and letting them know they are paying full attention.
3 Then, swap over so the listener can experience being heard and the speaker experience being the silent listener.
4 When you've each had two minutes using active listening, try it again with reflective listening, the listener repeating back and checking what's been said.
5 When you've each had a go, talk it over. How did it feel to be given a free rein, knowing you weren't going to be interrupted? How did it feel to use both active and reflective skills as listener, and have them used on you as speaker?

There is one exception to the 'make eye contact and give full attention' rule in active and reflective listening. Sometimes people – especially teenagers – find it easier to sidle up to you and have an important discussion when you're doing something else – cooking, washing-up and driving are favourite times. The point is that not feeling 'under the spotlight' can often help them be both honest and confiding, and able to hear what you have to say. But they still need you to observe all the other rules – letting them know you are listening, being encouraged to continue, having your attention. Keep your eyes on the washing-up or road, but give your attention to them as much as you possibly – and safely – can.

OPEN QUESTIONS

The third important strategy to help communication is using open questions. Open questions, as we saw in Chapter 1, are important mainly because they are the opposite of what can kill a conversation, a closed question. A closed question, remember, is one which can be answered by yes, no or just a grunt. In fact, not only does it not encourage more, it positively begs to be snapped off short with a one-word retort plus a period. With an open question, by contrast, we make sure that we encourage the other person to think about what they might say and answer as fully as possible.

A closed question might be 'Was work/school good today?' In that question, which can best be answered 'Yes/no/what?', is an assumption that it should have been good, an expectation that you ought to answer yes... and then what? We often feel annoyed when the people we love are monosyllabic or short, but sometimes it's the question that dictates the response. In contrast, an open question would be 'Tell me about your day!' You can't answer that with a yes or no and, while you could be brief, it also gives lots of scope for elaboration and explanation. Closed questions tend to steer the other person down the avenue of enquiry we've chosen. When you leave a question open you might be surprised what someone chooses to tell you, ask you and share with you.

Standing up for yourself

An important technique that allows you to stand up for your own views involves the use of 'I' statements.

'I' statements are all about being able to say what 'I want' and what 'I need'. One truly awful thing I was often told as a child was 'I want doesn't get...' In other words, asking for anything and particularly making it personal by saying 'I' was somehow arrogant, selfish, demanding and bad in all sorts of ways. If you 'wanted', you had to wait until someone decided you deserved it. And you certainly were not expected to stand up for or stand by your own words or your wishes.

For that reason, if we made a comment or a request it had to be expressed as a **'you' statement**. Instead of 'owning' feelings, by claiming them as our own and by standing up for ourselves, we're encouraged to hold them at arm's length: 'One feels like that, doesn't one?' 'That's how you do it, don't you?' When we're upset, instead of coming out and saying honestly 'I'm really upset at you' or 'I made a mistake and I feel bad about it', we say 'You're an idiot!' or 'Look what you made me do.' 'You' statements deny responsibility for angry or critical remarks by implying they belong to someone else: 'Everyone thinks it's your fault.'

We may use 'you' statements as a way of not being overwhelmed by anger or despair, but they seldom give the other person a chance to understand what we're upset about, how we feel or why, or give them an opportunity to make any changes. Instead of helping, they make the other person defensive and increase hostility and conflict.

In contrast, 'I' statements help the person speaking, and the person being spoken to, to be clear about what is really going on.

WHAT AN 'I' STATEMENT DOES

Using an 'I' statement respects the other person and their point of view. It helps you say what you feel and want, but avoids making the other person feel as if they are the problem. This makes it far easier for both of you to come up with a solution – they can feel part of the solution, not all of the problem – and to take responsibility and act positively. Above all, 'I' statements help you stand up and speak out. Learning how to use them can help you in the future not to have to feel regrets about speaking up, and can help you go back and redress any regrets about not having done so in the past.

It can take some time to get into the habit of using 'I' statements. Most of us have had a lifetime of being told it's selfish or big-headed to say 'I'. But the more you use them, the more you'll find they work and help you and the other person feel good about the exchange.

An 'I' statement...

▶ describes the behaviour you are finding difficult

▶ explains the effect it has on you

▶ tells the other person how you feel about it

▶ invites them to join you in finding a solution.

For example:

'When you criticize me I feel really upset and angry. I feel put down because you don't ask me my side of the situation and I feel you're not listening to me. I'd like you to tell me what you feel is the problem but to do it adult to adult so that we can discuss it. If you're having a problem with that, let's talk about it.'

Or you might want to say:

'When I was little you used to criticize me in a way that made me feel useless. I felt really upset and angry and it has held me back. I want you to know how unpleasant it was and I would like to know if you have anything to say to me now.'

You may not get the apology you'd like, or have the other person recognize or appreciate what you felt. What, however, they cannot do when you use an 'I' statement is argue with what you say. They can argue with a 'you' statement because they can say 'No, I didn't say that or mean that.' When you say 'I feel', that's it: you feel. Any denial – 'No, you don't' or 'But we only meant...' or 'That's foolish!' – can simply be met by a further insistence on your part – 'That how I felt/feel.' What using 'I' statements can do is turn any conflict into discussion. An 'I' statement, by respecting your own opinion and your right to it, respects the other person's point of view and their ability and willingness to negotiate and compromise.

When you use an 'I' statement, you are:

▶ specific about what you want or feel, wanted or felt

▶ given the chance to recognize and say how you feel

- able to help other people understand what you want
- clear, honest and direct
- able to make your point without blaming, criticizing or judging other people.

Remember this: Points to consider

- Many regrets are caused, and continue to be a burden, because of a lack of proper communication.

- We all tend to assume far too much in our relationships rather than clearly telling others what we really feel.

- Everyone can improve their communication skills. You can use the strategies given in this chapter to do so.

Do you communicate?

Speaking up and standing up for what you say, mean and feel relies on being able to communicate. Using the strategies of listening, asking open questions and being able to use 'I' statements all help you do so. Communication is always two-way – you give as much as you take on board – and is far more than an exchange of information such as when you're getting home tonight, or instructions such as how to turn on the washing machine! It's about building bonds and staying in touch by sharing feelings and thoughts. Try the following self-assessment to see how well you communicate with those around you.

Self-assessment: How well do you communicate?

	Disagree strongly	Disagree	Not sure	Agree	Agree strongly
When I was young it was OK in my family to talk about our feelings or about what we thought.					
In my family now we can talk about what we feel and think.					

The people I live with tell me what they feel.					
The people I live with tell me what they think.					
We discuss our feelings in our family.					
I feel close to my partner and my family.					
We don't talk a lot, but I'm sure we just know what the other is thinking.					
I listen when the people close to me talk to me.					
The members of my family listen to me.					
I sometimes feel the people I live with don't listen to me.					
I can tell my partner anything.					
There are things I don't share with my partner.					
I feel my partner keeps some things from me.					
Everyone should have some secrets.					
Least said, soonest mended.					
I feel comfortable talking and listening to my partner and my family.					
The people I live with interrupt when I try to talk.					
I think I don't always give my full attention when the people I live with talk to me.					
My partner can do and say things that surprise me.					
When my partner is unhappy I usually know why.					
When I'm unhappy I can tell my partner why.					
There are certain subjects we avoid.					

There are no 'right' or 'wrong' answers. You can do this exercise on your own, and then consider what your answers may be telling you. Or you might do it with your family and then discuss together what the results say to you.

Top tips for improving your communication skills

▶ **Don't censor yourself.** So often, we don't speak up because we think of something to say and them immediately think of a reason to say quiet: 'I'm sure everyone else will have thought of that', 'It's a silly or an obvious idea', 'Everyone will laugh', 'What if they then ask questions and I go tongue-tied?' Yes, but what if it's exactly what everyone needs to hear, and what if they all benefit and what if they ask questions and you find you know just what to say? The worst option is not if you speak and it's wrong. The worst option is if you don't speak and you were right.

▶ **Don't underestimate yourself.** You are capable of more than you realize. You can attempt more, do more and achieve more. How do I know? Because most of us underestimate ourselves. We evade, we prevaricate, we avoid. Being arrogant and unrealistically optimistic may be neither attractive nor useful, but most of us would do better to up our expectations of ourselves just a little. And then, with each success, you could increase your assumptions about what you might try.

▶ **Accept compliments.** Next time anyone gives you a compliment, stop yourself saying what you probably always say – 'Oh, it was nothing', 'I'm sure anyone could have done it', 'No, no, it wasn't me, really.' Next time, say 'Thank you!' and smile. Refusing compliments isn't modest – it's ungracious. It implies that the person who noticed your efforts or your skill had it wrong. So next time, accept the pat on the back and award yourself a point.

▶ **Silence the voice in your head.** We tend to criticize ourselves far more than anyone else does, and usually because we have been criticized in the past. We internalize that criticism – we hear the voice of the person who made it, and replay it again and again so it becomes our voice, too. Accept realistic and positive analyses of your actions so you might do better, but next time you just hear carping and complaining, and anything that simply seeks to pull you down and make you feel bad, silence it.

▷ **Be spontaneous.** Thinking carefully before you act – 'looking before you leap' – is sound advice when it comes to investing money. But often thinking too carefully about emotional issues simply ties you up and holds you back until the moment has passed. If you feel like kissing or hugging someone you love, don't stifle the urge because people are watching or the situation seems inappropriate. Hold back enough times and it's not just that the moment passes – you get out of the habit. Tell yourself you should be doing important tasks instead of running through the snow or playing with your child (or partner!) and one of these days you'll wake up to the fact that you've grown too old, grown apart or lost them. As the poet Robert Herrick said:

> Gather ye rosebuds while ye may,
> Old Time is still a-flying;
> And this same flower that smiles today,
> Tomorrow will be dying.

Your Action Plan: Step 4 – consider your relationships

Step 4 of the Action Plan is to look at how you deal with relationships – past, present and future.

Research suggests that we value our intimate, family and friendship relationships above everything – they are usually rated as more important than money, career success or status. Yet some relationships, in the past or continuing now, leave us with serious regrets. This may be because we put more emphasis on what other people thought of us than what we thought of ourselves. Even when and if the people around us are supportive and sympathetic, it is important that we learn how to trust ourselves and think for ourselves. Paul says:

'I've always been someone who needed to hear what other people thought. It has handicapped me in some ways because I feel really nervous about putting forward my own views first, and I can't enjoy success unless I hear positive feedback from somebody else. Someone recently said you can get like that if you've had too much praise as a child – it's as if you get addicted to always hearing praise and can't do without it, and that rang bells with me. I always thought my parents were great because I couldn't eat a biscuit without being told I was doing it beautifully. Which is why I was puzzled as to why I was so fearful and lacking in confidence. I think it's true – I can't praise myself because I've never had the chance.'

It's even more important when the people around us were less than supportive. As one respondent to my questionnaire said:

'While I find it hard to approve of the way some of my friends let their children rule the household, at the back of my mind I do think those children (especially the girls) are being listened to and bolstered; they aren't endlessly being told to be quiet, that their opinions don't count, that they should do as they are told.'

And, more graphically, Val said:

'All I can remember about my childhood was the relentless bullying. My brothers followed my parents' example and hit me, swore at me, told me I was a waste of space. I had a string of boyfriends who did the same – I think I picked them because quite frankly I didn't know any other type or way of relating. It wasn't until I met my first husband that I found people didn't have to be that way but the damage had been done – I had no confidence or feelings of self-worth and it really poisoned my life.'

The biggest postbag I get as an agony aunt is probably about 'toxic relationships' – relationships that are either with partners, family or friends, that do you no good whatsoever.

WE DON'T ALWAYS AGREE

Healthy relationships can have conflict. We don't always agree and we might sometimes argue. That's understandable – we all have our own needs and viewpoints, and we can't either know what the other person is thinking, feeling or needing, or necessarily be wanting the same thing. What you do in a healthy relationship is talk it through – both put your own side, listen to the other person's, and by compromise and negotiation come up with a situation where both of you get some of what you want. In a healthy relationship you care about the other person, you want them to be pleased and happy, but you care about yourself, too. Neither you, nor they, want either of you to win out over the other, or to sacrifice themselves. It's called a win/win situation – both of you win rather than one winning and the other losing, or indeed both losing because you've argued so much the whole situation falls apart.

> **Key idea:** You can't be perfect
>
> We can't all be perfect all the time and sometimes you lose it and shout or slam doors. That's human nature and both understandable and forgivable, as long as it's the exception to your general rule of discussing, negotiating and compromising.

RETURNING THE FAVOUR

Relationships between adults need to be reciprocal – each gives and takes in equal measure. Not always at the same time – one of you can be down and the other person is caring and supportive and puts their own needs to the side for a time. But the understanding is that at some point in the future, the situation will be reversed or you'll go back to being jointly considerate. It's also understandable that the situation can be uneven depending on the age of the people in the relationship. Parents care for their children, giving them not only unconditional love but also an unequal share of being looked after. When parents do not make their children feel accepted, loved and secure, or indeed demand from them that they care for their parents, there is an imbalance and it is harmful, and toxic. This is where children are left struggling with later relationships, because they have neither a secure foundation nor a healthy model on which to base their own adult relationships.

Remember this: Points to consider

▶ Using the self-assessment exercise will tell you how well you communicate at the moment and what you can do to improve things.

▶ Using the Action Plan will guide you into seeing how to deal with all your relationships – past, present and future.

▶ 'Toxic' relationships need to be recognized for what they are, and be dealt with.

▶ Healthy relationships are all about give and take. Genuinely caring for each other makes even an argument into a win/win situation.

Key idea: What 'mutual support' means in the family

Don't get me wrong about mutual support, by the way – this isn't a 'get out of jail free' card when it comes to doing chores round the home! Children should most certainly be brought up learning how to care for themselves and others and be asked to do chores. But that's not the same as taking on the adult or parental role in a family.

'Toxic' relationships

So often, when family relationships were toxic, this leads to people accepting unsupportive intimate relationships as an adult, and friendships, too. Carrie said:

> 'I have this friend I've known since school. Well, I call her a friend but, to be honest, she really depresses me. She always moans and moans about her life and expects me to come up with ideas to make it better, but rubbishes every suggestion I have. Oh – and when I was ill last year she suddenly had a family crisis and couldn't be in touch. But she was back as soon as I was well. We always have to do what she wants and she'll pour cold water on any suggestion of mine even

when she knows it's something I'd really like to do. I recently met a man I like so much and she's on and on at me to dump him – she says he'll only dump me soon, like her last guy did. But he's not like that! I wish I could stop being friends but she just rings me up and assumes we'll go out together.'

Key idea: Don't put up with toxic friends

Putting up with a toxic friend does you and your family no good and it does the 'friend' no good either. The more you accept bad behaviour the more you reinforce it; your acceptance tells the other person that what they are doing is OK.

WHAT DO YOU DO ABOUT TOXIC RELATIONSHIPS?

Recognize that the past affects your present and future. So many regrets come about because we follow patterns laid down for us in our early lives. The examples we saw in our own family about how you relate and react to other people, and the assumptions you make about yourself and others, all come from your past and echo through your present to your future. To go forward with confidence, we often do need to lay the past to rest and we may need to explore and examine it to do so.

▶ **Get rid of their influence.** Carrie, with her demanding and selfish friend, realized that, before she could tackle what to do about this woman, she first had to recognize why she had such a hold. Carrie remembered how her mother had drilled into her that she had to be polite. When she was asked to do something she had to do it, even if she really didn't want to – such as accept an invitation to a play-date with a girl who bullied her at school. Or kiss her uncle, when she really didn't want to get within a hand's reach of him. 'No' was rude, and 'no' was not allowed in a home where Carrie's views, feelings and thoughts were not invited and were discounted. Carrie loved her mother but came to see that she could shrug off much of her influence without rejecting her outright. She could say: 'I love you. You were wrong to refuse to listen to me. I will trust my own feelings in future.'

▶ **It wasn't your fault.** One part of the influence that can have you regretting past relationships and struggling with present and future ones is that you blame yourself for what might have gone wrong. Children find it very hard to recognize that their parents are human and fallible. When parents act carelessly, selfishly or even cruelly, children tend to imagine it was their own fault – they did something wrong, they were unworthy, they brought it on themselves. This can translate into the belief that adult relationships that are dysfunctional are also your own fault – you provoked the other into being violent or unfaithful or angry or uncaring. Children are never at fault when treated badly. Children can become badly behaved, but it's a reaction to the way they are treated. And, of course, adults can behave in ways that do not nurture a good relationship – but, if it's because of the way you were treated as a child, it's not your fault. It may become your responsibility when you have the opportunity to see what is going on and can take action. But berating yourself and accepting the idea that you deserve bad treatment – you do not have to accept that.

 Key idea

It's not what others think but what we think about ourselves that matters.

▶ **You don't have to forgive to let go.** Val, on the other hand, did not love her parents and was consumed with anger and resentment. What she did not want to do – understandably – was let them off the hook. What they had done was wrong, she felt, and could not be forgiven, but she recognized that her rage was holding her back and doing her immense harm. What she could accept finally was that they might have felt they were doing the right thing or simply did not realize what was happening, and that, while she would not forgive their actions, she would let go of her anger against them – if only because she was harming herself more than them. Her mother could not accept that she had done anything wrong, but Val's new quiet confidence led to a change in her relationship with them. Her mother made tentative attempts at being loving and her brothers, faced with a refusal by Val to rise to their teasing, finally began to treat her maturely. Best of all, having faced her family, Val developed her self-confidence and self-worth, met someone who would be her second husband and felt able to accept his kindness.

▶ **Say no**. Sometimes you have to take a long hard look at how you contribute to a situation you say you don't like. It's hard when you have been brought up to say yes and be polite and always put your own needs or views last. But often the most positive thing you can do is learn to say no. Consider the situation when a family member or friend calls you on the phone and consequently you're late for a meeting that you wanted to go to because 'They just wouldn't let me go!' How does that person keep you on the phone when they ring and you don't want to talk to them? Is your hand and ear glued to the receiver? No – you make the choice to keep on listening and answering. I'm not pretending it's easy to resist, but there comes a point when it's no longer your background that is to blame, it's you who are making that choice. And you no longer need to. The ability you need to cultivate is the ability to say no. You don't need to give explanations or even apologies – both imply that the other person has a right to your time. 'I have another commitment' / 'I don't have time to talk' / 'I'm going – goodbye!' are all that is needed. And that applies in relationships, too: 'I'm leaving' / 'We're over' / 'This is not working.'

▶ **Seek help**. You can't always do all this on your own. We still have, in this country, an unfortunate attitude that sees seeking professional counselling help as being weak or silly. The stigma is getting less, possibly because more and more people can testify to how effective and helpful it can be. You can find a counsellor through Relate, Family Lives and many more charities and through your own GP – there's more information in the Appendix. Seeking help and saying you have a problem are a sign of strength.

▶ **Look for new contacts**. If your past relationships are the source of your regrets, you cannot go back and change them then and there. We often try to do so by becoming involved in dysfunctional relationships that bear a strong resemblance to those in our past. If we had a violent or uncaring parent, we may well choose someone who acts in the same way. Not only do we do this because we don't know any better – this, we think, is what relationships are all about. We also gravitate towards someone like that because we mean to change them – the woman with the philandering father who chooses an unfaithful husband, the man with a cold mother who chooses a cold partner. We insist that they have a good side really and that we will bring it out. And, of course, all that happens is the same thing we experienced as children – heartache.

▶ But even if we were successful in 'saving' and redeeming' the partner, we cannot go back and change the person we really long to change, the parent. We can, however, go back in our understanding and let go of our anger and pain, and their influence. And what we can most certainly do is cease contact with people who hurt us, and look for new ones with whom we can have healthy relationships. It's not easy to go out and make new contacts – it was far easier in the early years of being in the highly charged and rapidly changing social situations of school, college and a first job. But the reality is we can – if we make the effort.

'The most important thing in life is to stop saying "I wish" and start saying "I will". Consider nothing impossible, then treat the possibilities as probabilities.'

Charles Dickens

Focus points

✻ Many, probably most, regrets revolve around communication – or lack of it!

✻ People are not mind-readers, so making assumptions about what they think is no substitute for telling them what you really think and feel, and asking them about their thoughts and feelings.

✻ Everyone can improve their communication skills to some degree. This can help us to express our true feelings, resolve conflicts – and limit future regrets.

✻ Active and reflective listening and 'I' and 'You' statements are tried-and-tested ways to promote better communication.

✻ Doing an honest self examination – or the self-assessment – will tell you where you are in the communication stakes at the moment.

✻ Your newly improved communication skills will help you deal with and resolve past, present and future relationships.

✻ Good, healthy, relationships depend on mutual caring and neither party wanting to 'score' over the other.

✻ The real aim of good communication in a relationship is to produce a win/win situation where nobody loses.

✻ We all have some 'toxic' relationships that will continue until we resolve them – with the techniques and strategies given in this chapter.

✻ If all else fails, seek help. There are a lot of effective and helpful charities, counsellors and GPs out there. Some of these are listed in the Appendix.

Next step

Money has an emotional weight and the way it is used can often lead to regret. The next chapter shows you how to control the money in your life and put money in its proper place.

6

'I wish I'd managed my money better'

In this chapter you will learn:

▶ *How coming from a poor background can leave you with later regrets*

▶ *How money can work in society – for good or bad or as a means of manipulation or control*

▶ *How money can have an emotional 'weight' that can both produce or relieve regrets*

▶ *How to control the money in your life – how to budget, and how to put money in its proper place for you.*

Being poor

Being poor can blight your life and chances. Several people answering my questionnaire said that their biggest regret had been 'being born into a poor family'. This a theme I've heard before, in therapy and in letters to my agony page. Such regrets didn't just revolve around lack of cash as a child, although poverty can lead to children feeling excluded and stigmatized. It can affect your self-confidence and sense of self-worth to feel you are the only one who doesn't have clothing and belongings that allow you to blend in with your peers. It's hard to know that you are one of the few unable to go on the school trips or join friends in activities. This feeling of being disqualified and labelled can last into adulthood. But being poor can also lead to a feeling that you grew up in a home where books and education were not valued and available:

> *'I so regret that I grew up with parents who just didn't "get" education. Books were a waste of time and homework was something to be laughed at and avoided – they'd certainly never dream of making any efforts to help me do mine or give me peace and quiet to get on with it. It wasn't seen, as I saw it from an early age, as a way of bettering myself. We earned what we earned because that was the way of the world – no point in trying otherwise.'*

Of course, that's not always the case – money and culture do not always go hand in hand, and not being able to afford books does not always mean that they and what they represent are not valued and sought after – that, after all, is what libraries are there for:

> *'My mother used to take me to our local library every Friday afternoon and I was allowed to borrow six books to tide me over till the next week. I got my own ticket on my 11th birthday and it was the best birthday present I ever had! I was the first in my family to go to university, the first to earn a salary rather than a wage. I don't regret growing up poor because it's made me work all the harder for what I now have, and I'm grateful to my parents for helping me on my way.'*

Money's place in our society

Money has a curious place in our society. It's a symbol of value – awarded to you as earnings for work done or accrued in various ways that can be felt to be prudent or clever. We give higher status in our culture to people who have lots of money, whether from their salaries or from family or inherited wealth. Money is valuable and it is valued. And it is also value in itself. Those higher salaries ostensibly go to people who have 'earned it' – by getting qualifications, having greater skill or talents, or working harder than most. More money says 'I'm better', which then means that someone earning plenty can have the status even if by anybody's standards what they actually do is of a lesser need to society than what is done by someone on less pay. Indeed, such status can be given even to people who do things that many feel are harmful. They are still admired, as long as they are rich.

> **Key idea: Money can be a substitute**
>
> So often, whether in families or at work, money stands in for respect and value, love and attention.

Money as a means of control or manipulation

We often use money to convey approval or affection. Young children may feel pleased to have more presents than a sibling at birthdays or festivals, and even count them to see if they've been slighted or elevated. Older children may be acutely aware of how much things cost, and feel deflated or elated if they feel they've been given as much or less than those around them, as if this proves they are loved. This is often what 'pester power' is all about – it's the demand to be noticed and be approved of. But the reality is that, while we may know the monetary value of the goods, what we are really seeking is attention and approval – in other words, to be told we are valued and of worth. The bigger the price ticket, the more worthwhile we may feel we are to the person who gave to us. After all, isn't that what we see in society around us?

We also withhold money to send a different message or to be controlling or manipulative. I often get letters to my agony page like the one I received from Tony, who said:

'I don't know whether we should talk to a lawyer but my wife and I, for the last ten years, have been the ones to look after her ailing father. It's taken up time, for which she gets no thanks, and costs us money. I wouldn't mind but he's demanding and abusive to her, and all he can talk about is her two brothers, who do nothing and hardly ever bother to come and see him. Now we've been told that in his will he's left them just about everything and she gets a derisory amount of cash. Is there anything I can do to make sure she gets her just deserts?'

On a similar theme, Emma wrote to say:

'My youngest son was so close to me when he was a child but in the last few years has been distant and even heartless. When I was ill last year he hardly came to see me, and I know his brother and sister have had arguments with him about it. They have steady, responsible jobs and families while he is what my mother would have called a wastrel. We're redoing our wills to take into account our grandchildren and I'm ashamed to say I'm tempted to leave him a lot less than his siblings. Can I do that?'

Case study: Becca

As long as she could remember, Becca's mother set her children against each other, was manipulative, cold and even, on occasion, violent. She'd also dole out pocket money haphazardly, to keep her children at each others' throats. Becca left home as soon as she could and ignored her mother's frequent demands for visits and help, and the threats of being cut out of her will if Becca didn't do as she was told. When the day finally came, as she had expected, there was nothing for Becca. But, as she said, she'd made her own happy family, earned her own living and had long ago resigned herself the fact that her mother would give her nothing – neither money nor love and attention. She didn't look to cash to be the way her mother might redress her failings, so being denied it didn't hurt or otherwise upset her.

A belief that poverty was a bad beginning may not be justified. It's worth noting that being rich may be just as destructive as being poor. Recent research suggests that people with a lot of money often don't have productive social engagements or networks. Whether people who strive to make money then neglect to make friendships, or whether people who find it hard to establish emotional entanglements seek to make money to make up for it, might be debatable!

The emotional 'weight' of money

Recognizing what emotional weight we put on money can help you put some regrets into perspective. Once you can see the link that we often make between money and love, and recognize that the two are in fact different issues, it might be helpful if you can separate them. People might indeed use their money to make emotional points, but you don't have to take it that way. Charlie says:

> 'We had three years of our children writing out ever more demanding "gimme lists" for Christmas and birthdays. Last year we were paying the credit card bills until the summer and we still had sulks and tantrums on the day. Then I read something that made me think about how we were in our family. Their dad worked long hours and never saw them and I spent half my time at home on my mobile. So we made real efforts to spend time with them. I made new rules about switching phones off and limiting the amount of time we all spent on computers and watching TV. My husband kept to his work hours instead of being late in the office every day, and he'd read them bedtime stories and stuff. Last Christmas we said we'd get them what we thought was right – no lists. And we bought board games and gave them vouchers for days out with them, sometimes Mum or Dad on their own with them and some as a family. It was brilliant – it was voted the best Christmas ever. They're insisting birthdays should be the same. So it worked!'

Try it now: How do you use money?

Ask yourself how you use money. Do the following statements apply to you? To what degree?

* My pay packet reflects my worth.
* I'm proud, or embarrassed, to let people know what I earn.
* If I didn't have a job that paid me, I'd feel diminished.
* I spend more on presents for people I like.
* If I needed to apologize or make up for something, I'd buy a present.
* I buy myself something when I need cheering up or rewarding.
* If I don't get a salary increase, I feel my work hasn't been noted.
* Working for less money would mean my skills were less valued.

Now consider these thoughts:

* I know what my skills and abilities are – my salary doesn't necessarily reflect all of them.
* Saying 'please', 'sorry', 'thank you' and 'I love you' are worth more than cash.
* My friends and family know and like me for who I am.
* The thought that goes into a gift is worth more than the gift.

There are no right or wrong answers; this is simply a chance to think your way through how money is used and how getting our use of it into perspective might help.

Putting money in its proper place

Putting money in its place can be transformational. There can be no doubt that knowing how to budget, how to save and how to prioritize what you do to earn, and how you spend, your money can help considerably in staving off regrets. One questionnaire respondent said her chief regret had been 'not having forced myself to save more while I could', while another said:

> 'I'm semi-retired now but can't be fully retired as some of my friends because I never put anything into a private pension. I have the state one and that's all so I have to go on earning. Do I regret that? Yes, but I have to face up to the fact I made the choice to be a grasshopper rather than an ant. I spent it and enjoyed it. Maybe I wouldn't have enjoyed my time any less if I'd put just a small amount away but we really didn't think we had enough to do that, back in the day.'

Case study: Saul

Saul feels some resentment towards his parents for never having introduced the subject of budgets and savings when he was small. 'I had friends whose parents insisted they put some of their birthday money and pocket money into savings and I thought that was very boring. I got quite generous handouts when I needed or wanted them, but there was never any discussion of how to manage money. And, unlike most of my friends, as I grew older I didn't have an allowance. It's quite odd really because my parents have three pensions each and are now very comfortably off as retirees, whereas I'm hopeless with money. If it wasn't for the fact that my employers insist on a workplace pension I wouldn't be paying into one. My dad recently said that he felt bad about the fact that they hadn't been more helpful. Part of me says it's a bit bloody late now and yes, I wish you had! Part of me acknowledges that it's now my own responsibility and I can't go on blaming them for my deficiencies.'

Knowing how to budget, manage and save money is certainly something that should start in childhood. Studies suggest that many young people today enter adult life with some very sketchy ideas of how to manage their money. According to a survey for Barclays, almost half may not know how to tell the difference on a bank statement between being in credit and being overdrawn – in fact, around one in eight didn't even know what an overdraft was. And, most worryingly, more than a quarter did not understand what an APR (annual percentage rate) was, or know that it would be better to opt for a lower than a higher one when taking out a credit card or a loan.

The rise of so-called 'payday loan' companies, in particular, shows a terrifying lack of understanding about how much you can find yourself paying for a loan. These trade on the idea that, if you find yourself short at the end of the month and need a small amount to tide you over a few days, you can borrow it easily and pay it back when you get paid, with a 'small' payment for the privilege. This payment of course leaves you even more short at the end of the next month, and so on. If you don't understand APR and are only looking at the fact that you could get £200 for a week and pay a fee of £20, you might miss the fact that if you default – or as they call it 'roll over' – you're paying interest at a rate of up to, and sometimes beyond, 4,000 per cent over a year. That's why some customers can start with a £100 loan and end up owing £17,000.

Money and the young

The best beginning in money management is to receive 'pocket money' to spend from an early age, but for there to be some expectations to go with it. Before deciding on how much you give your children, you need to clarify what the pocket money is supposed to be for. Is it just to spend on what they want – if so, it's worth noting that over 30 per cent of pocket money is spent on sweets and chocolate. Will you have any input into what they do with it? It's estimated that 29 per cent of boys and 20 per cent of girls spend all their money in the week that they get it. The key is that children who see pocket money as a give-and-take situation – you give them money but they are also expected to do their share of chores – do much better later in life.

Expecting them also to save some of the cash they receive, and to use it to buy or contribute to larger items they want, or to buy their own presents for friends or family, also sets up good habits for later in life. Primary school children can manage this situation, having an average of between £2.50 to £3 a week from a variety of sources that may be parents, grandparents and other family members.

Once children go to secondary school, an allowance may be a better way of teaching them how to manage their money. The allowance means more cash, but with strings. You might give them a weekly, monthly or even quarterly amount, in cash or paid into a bank account or building society, a credit or savings account. With it goes the understanding that they are now responsible for certain of their expenses. You might want to start by handing over to them the responsibility for out-of-school travel and entertainment – an agreed amount to cover going to see their friends or visiting cinemas, for buying games, downloads or DVDs and books. You may want to give them an agreed amount for their mobile phone, but insist they always keep minutes back for emergencies.

You may want to give them responsibility for all or some non-school clothes. You may want to start small and, as they demonstrate good practice, increase the money and the areas they can be in charge of.

> **Key idea:** It pays to start early
>
> The earlier we begin to learn how to handle money wisely, the better we will be at budgeting and managing our finances.

And, most importantly of all, you will have to stand firm if they blow it. They may need a safety net in some cases, but the principle should be that they won't learn if you bail them out. So if your adolescent spends an entire entertainment budget for a month on a concert and then can't go to the cinema with friends – tough. Earn it or miss out. If they spend the whole clothing allowance on a new pair of boots, and then need a new pair of jeans – tough. Make do with an old pair or go search the charity shops. If you made similar spending choices, you'd face the same consequence, so it's a learning experience. It may be hard for you to maintain, but it's vital for them to learn.

Money and the nearly-adult

As apprentice adults, young people rise to responsibility and they need to learn how to handle cash now while they have your guidance and a safety net, rather than putting it off until they are on their own and can court disaster, as perhaps you did. Young people need to see that money can be divided into three sections:

1 money to be spent now on pleasing yourself

2 money that has to pay regular bills

3 money that should be saved for future needs – unforeseen bills, holidays, presents for other people, and so on.

Teenagers tend to be big on the first section, especially because that's the way they began with pocket money. Some children learn from example to put money away, saving up for Christmas and birthday presents for family and friends, or for an item they want and know they have to buy for themselves or contribute to. But the second section is the one they may find hard to visualize, because that's what parents do for them. It may then be the financial aspect they fail on, when they go independent for the first time.

As a parent, you can help your teenager gain control over their future as well as present finances by setting up a system that gives them an income but which also requires them to handle it. You can help them by explaining your own budget – where money comes from, how you spend it. Nothing quite knocks on the head the fantasy that Mum and Dad could give them everything they wanted if only you weren't so mean, as showing them bills and explaining how many hours you need to work to pay them.

And it helps to get them into the habit of seeing work as part of the way a family runs. Mum and Dad aren't servants doing everything – they have to muck in, too, starting as small children clearing up their toys then keeping their bedrooms tidy then washing up or loading dishwashers, folding laundry, vacuuming, feeding pets and dusting. You might want to tie early pocket money and later some of their allowance into the satisfactory completion of chores, or agree extras such as mowing lawns or washing cars as being paid chores.

This can prepare them for going outside to earn money from someone other than you. Children who get a job outside the home as soon as they can are the ones who grow up managing money best of all. It has to be legal, however, and safe. In the UK, children can work for pay from the age of 13, with certain provisos. They can work during term time but only up to 12 hours a week. This includes:

➤ a maximum of 2 hours on schooldays and Sundays

➤ a maximum of 5 hours on Saturdays for 13- to 14-year-olds, or 8 hours for 15- to 16-year-olds.

During school holidays they can work a maximum of 25 hours a week if they are aged 13 to 14. This includes:

- a maximum of 5 hours on weekdays and Saturdays
- a maximum of 2 hours on Sunday.

If they are aged 15 to 16, they can work up to 35 hours a week during school holidays. This includes:

- a maximum of 8 hours on weekdays and Saturdays
- a maximum of 2 hours on Sunday.

Children are not allowed to work:

- without an employment permit issued by the education department of the local council, if this is required by local bylaws
- in places like a factory or industrial site
- during school hours
- before 7 a.m. or after 7 p.m.
- for more than one hour before school (unless local bylaws allow it)
- for more than 4 hours without taking a break of at least 1 hour
- in most jobs in pubs and betting shops and those prohibited in local bylaws
- in any work that may be harmful to their health, wellbeing or education
- without having a 2-week break from any work during the school holidays in each calendar year.

Money and regrets

Many people have regrets that revolve around the money they have, the money they might have spent unwisely and the money they may have received or given away. Seeing how you might help your children manage money better often helps you see where you might have gone astray. Is it too late to seize back control if you feel that early money mismanagement caused you problems, and continues to do so?

Doing the above exercise, considering our money as being divisible into those three sections, often puts it into perspective. It can be quite scary to realize how much we need to put aside for sections 2 and 3, and therefore how little we actually have for section 1. The reality is that we often do risk section 2 and skimp on section 3 to treat ourselves. But, sometimes, that's a reasoned choice and a good one. We need to know when it is both permissible and indeed downright necessary to splurge and break the bank, to do something or get something that otherwise would leave us for ever regretting it. 'We spent an ISA on a painting we saw, that strongly reminded us of our honeymoon,' one couple told me. 'We knew without a doubt we'd have regretted it for ever if we hadn't!'

How to make and balance a budget

It can help to take yourself through a budget template – a list of all possible expenses you have. Taking your children through one is vital for them as teenagers, not only for them to see what money you have and where it goes, but for you to be then able to discuss exactly why you are so horribly 'mean' and 'miserly' to them. A few home truths make the point better than a row caused by your simply saying no to a new games console. But even if you haven't got children, it's a very useful exercise.

The point is that, once you can see on paper how much you have and exactly where it goes, you can make changes if needed or if you so choose. You can, for instance, divide expenses into essential and discretionary, and have the debate about what goes where. Faced with the actual figures, sometimes things you felt were essential to a civilized life become an unnecessary burden. Quite a few people I know have found the incentive to give up smoking when faced with the truly horrific amount they had been spending on it. The following exercise provides a useful template to help you budget.

Try it now: Fill in a budget template

WHAT'S COMING IN

What you earn from your work (after tax and contributions, what you actually have left) _____

Any benefits or credits _____

Any other money _____

Money coming in _____

WHAT YOU'RE SPENDING

Rent/mortgage _____

Council tax _____

Water rates _____

Electricity/gas _____

Other fuel _____

Phone, broadband, TV licence, entertainment packages (e.g. Sky) and downloads _____

Food and household items _____

Alcohol _____

Smoking _____

Travel incl. all car expenses – fuel, tax, insurance _____

Childcare _____

Clothing/shoes _____

Haircuts _____

Papers/magazines/books _____

Christmas/birthdays/holidays _____

Entertainment/going out _____

Insurances _____

Credit cards _____

Store cards _____

Mail order/catalogues _____

Other _____

Savings _____

Total you spend _____

The key, then, is getting your attitudes to money into perspective. Do you have resentments and grief from the way it was used when you were younger? Was that about opportunities denied, or about affection withheld? And how has it affected you? Do you have areas in your life you'd like to go back and address – education or training you felt you didn't have access to then but might be able to catch up on now? Or might you want to go back and challenge people for the way they used money to withhold other things? And would you far prefer to face up to the way this legacy has made you feel or even act yourself, and change that? It's never too late to make your own changes.

> 'Annual income twenty pounds, annual expenditure nineteen pounds nineteen shillings and six pence, result happiness. Annual income twenty pounds, annual expenditure twenty pounds ought and six, result misery.'
>
> Mr Micawber in Charles Dickens's *David Copperfield*

Remember this: Points to consider

▶ Money can carry a considerable emotional 'weight'.

▶ Putting money in its proper place in your life should be a priority.

▶ Starting to teach the young about money at an early age can avoid their making mistakes and having regrets in the future.

▶ Everyone should learn how to budget and to control their money through life.

▶ Money may not be the root of all evil, but it is at the centre of many regrets.

Your Action Plan: Step 5 – grieve for your regrets

In earlier stages of your Action Plan you identified your regrets and said sorry to yourself and others for what led to them. You have also addressed how some relationships can be toxic and considered how to deal with that. Step 5 of your Action Plan is to grieve for your regrets.

Grieving is something many cultures understand, but which other cultures think of as unnecessary, embarrassing or even counterproductive. In the buttoned-up UK, for instance, the view seems to be that crying is discomforting, and people will go out of their way to avoid showing tears or provoking them. Anyone who has suffered a loss will tell you this. Greg said to me:

'I was astonished how many of our friends went out of their way to avoid me when we were mourning. They'd cross the road so they wouldn't have to say anything and when we came face to face, they'd avoid the subject.'

We seem to feel that raising the issue causes the grief for which they don't want to feel responsible, rather than it allowing a display of feelings we have anyway. And some people will go to great lengths to hide their feelings, thinking that they are doing the right thing. Greg recognized this:

'We didn't handle it very well ourselves, of course. We were pleased with ourselves that we didn't break down in front of our children and shielded them from the worst of it. What we hadn't understood was that this meant they felt we didn't care, and they couldn't come to us for comfort because they thought we wouldn't understand. We just thought they were handling it well.'

Key idea: Communicate your grief

While you may not wish to burden other people with your feelings, it doesn't help anyone for you to hide them. How can people know what you feel unless you say, and how can they help unless you are open and clear?

In many cultures, mourning is a well-formulated ritual. People know when something terrible happens that it's OK to weep, wail, rend their clothing. Gatherings may be held to allow everyone to express their sadness and obtain comfort. Obviously, we're talking on the whole here about the grief that comes when people die. But it does mean that the society has an acceptance of tears as being not only a normal part of life but as healing in themselves. Often, we need to mourn to have a chance of leaving regrets behind and getting past them. We need a chance to do that crying and indeed that complaining, to say 'Why me?' and 'It's so unfair!' and have it heard and accepted by ourselves and those with whom we wish to share our feelings. If we don't mourn, we get stuck endlessly rehashing the same problem or situation.

So how do you fully grieve for those regrets or what they led to, before moving on to make a new beginning? Sometimes we have to overcome our natural reticence and embarrassment and carry out a mourning ritual that will allow us the chance to regroup.

A mourning ritual allows you two things. By setting out to experience one it can help you to recognize how much something has affected you. Until you allow yourself to consider grieving you might not have realized that you have something to grieve over, and that may be exactly what is holding you back. Let's consider the seven stages of grief:

The process of grieving

Grief is not just sadness. When something awful happens to you, you go through a process:

1 At first you feel shock and denial – you can't believe it happened, and try to pretend it didn't.
2 Then you might feel pain and guilt – guilt that it might have been your fault, that there was something you could have done or not done to stop this happening.
3 Then you might feel anger – at yourself, or at whoever caused your grief.
4 You may try bargaining – promising to do or not do something in the hope that this will reverse the situation.
5 Depression may follow, and loneliness, as you feel alone in your grief.
6 Eventually, having passed through those stages, you begin to reconstruct your life and work through your feelings.
7 Finally, you reach acceptance and hope.

Key idea: Grief is a process...

Grief is a process and it can take some time for us to go through it.

Everyone goes through these stages, in some order and at some time. You might skip one stage only to go back to it, rush through one to get snarled up on another, or find yourself redoing one particular stage several times. You can see, however, that to reach acceptance and hope you do need to pass through the others. What mires us in regrets so often is that we get stuck in one stage and can't move past it – whether it is anger, guilt or depression. And that's why a mourning ritual can help because it focuses your mind on several things:

▶ It's normal to feel grief over past regrets.

▶ It's OK to mourn.

▶ Mourning is cathartic.

So what can you do to bring your feelings out, and move past them? You can do several things:

▶ **Set the scene** The Victorians did know how to mourn – conspicuously. They'd dress in black, cover mirrors and withdraw from public view. You might like to put on the trappings and drape black around the house, to get yourself into the mood.

▶ **Set the table** In some cultures, a farewell feast is created that can include symbolic foods such as eggs, which represent continuing life. You might like to signify your intentions by treating yourself and anyone accompanying you to your favourite foods, symbolic of your intention to look after yourself and move on.

▶ **Set up a farewell** The intention is to move you on from your regrets and from anger, guilt or sadness. Consider what it is that you'd like to leave behind, or anything you might like to say to yourself or others but haven't been able to do so. Then write it down, as fully as possible. You could scribble on a piece of scrap paper or write it beautifully on headed notepaper in ink. You could tap it out on a laptop and then print it out, in Arial or an elaborate typeface, or even using something you can't read such as Aparajita or Wingbats. Outside, in a garden or on a patio, or in a park or on open land, set up a small fire or barbeque or candle. Reflect on your regret and then burn the piece of paper. As the paper turns to ash and crumbles and the smoke ascends, say goodbye to your regrets and let them go.

▶ **Wash your hands of it** Washing has always been part of some mourning rituals. Sometimes it's a means of purifying the participants so that they can take part. But it can also be used as a way of signalling that you quite literally 'wash your hands' of the issue. You could make your bathroom the scene of your ritual, setting up candles everywhere, using scented soap and a drop of scented oil in the water. Or, if you want to do it with family and friends, you might like to do it in a larger room with a pretty bowl. Use warmed, soft and fluffy towels and afterwards scented hand cream to finish the job.

Remember this: Points to consider

▶ Grieving for our regrets is necessary, but in this society it is often thought to be not needed.

▶ Sometimes we will have to overcome natural reticence or embarrassment before we can begin the grieving process.

▶ Grieving is now a well-understood process and you should be aware of and accept its stages before you set off on your own journey.

Top tips

▶ **Count your blessings.** Noticing and adding up the good things in your life, rather than bemoaning and focusing on the bad, makes you less likely to have regrets. It really helps if you acknowledge and celebrate any positive aspects and use that recognition to get negatives into perspective.

▶ **Be positive.** Do you see those little, natural, everyday drawbacks as problems or as challenges to be overcome, opportunities to seize, tasks to be done and tests passed? Approaching small setbacks in a positive frame of mind gives you the tools to tackle the bigger issues the same way. The more positive you are, the fewer regrets you will have.

Focus points

✳ Lack of early money can be an easy excuse for later failure. Early poverty and its effects should be examined closely before they are given all the blame for later regrets.

✳ Money has a very mixed role in our society. It can be used for both good and bad – to assist, reward or inspire, or to manipulate, punish or control.

✳ Money can have a considerable emotional 'weight' and putting money into its proper place in your life can save you from unnecessary regrets.

✳ Money management is all-important. Everyone should learn how to budget and how to control their money.

✳ Teaching the young about money at as early an age as possible, and continuing through childhood and adolescence, should help to make them happier and less potentially regretful adults.

✳ Money cannot be blamed for everything, but there is no doubt that it is at the centre of many regrets.

✳ The need to grieve is something that most cultures understand. In the West, we have often been brought up to view grief as unnecessary.

✳ Sometimes we need to get rid of instilled reticence and embarrassment before we can begin to grieve.

✳ There is now a good understanding of grief. It is a definite and predictable process and you should be aware of its likely stages before setting out on your own journey.

✳ Whether you are dealing with money or grief, the message is the same – be grateful for what you have and be positive about what you are going to do.

Next step

The next chapter looks at the quality of our relationships and how to make them work so that their failure is not a cause of later regret.

7

'I wish I'd thought about my relationships better'

In this chapter you will learn:

▶ *How love, sex and relationships can be the biggest causes of life's problems – and regrets*

▶ *Why self-confidence is necessary if you are to make and keep relationships*

▶ *Ten ways to help make a relationship work*

▶ *How to understand your feelings, resolve arguments and accept change.*

Intimate relations

Our loving and intimate relationships are probably the most important things in our lives. Research suggests that people put more value on these than they do on having money or status. If your love life is right, everything is right. If it's problematical, then, however successful you may seem in other areas, there will be something missing. Probably the biggest postbag I get as an agony aunt, in common with most problem-page columnists and most counsellors, revolves around respondents' love and sex lives. Being in a relationship that seems to offer little by way of care or support, getting married too early, marrying for the wrong reasons, paying more attention to the wedding day than the marriage itself, having children too quickly… all can leave you with regrets.

As the respondents to my questionnaire variously said, they regretted:

> 'Getting married – hideous mistake. Not getting married itself but the choice of husband.'

> 'Marrying the wrong person and not having a career.'

> 'Staying with a man who didn't love me and feeling humiliated afterwards when it ended.'

Another stated:

> 'If only I had lived with my former husband (which my parents wouldn't have approved of) rather than marrying him, I would have found it so much easier to extricate myself from that bad relationship.'

Others feel that they were the one who harmed someone else:

> 'I regret breaking someone's heart. Just over a year ago my boyfriend of seven years proposed, but it was just not the right thing for me and I broke up with him. I don't regret that decision, but I regret that I caused so much pain to someone I cared for deeply. Looking back, perhaps I should have been braver and said that things weren't working for me earlier on. I might have spared him and myself some heartache and not kept the relationship going for the length it did.'

Case study: Jeremy and Jacqui (part 1)

Jeremy and Jacqui came to see me because their ten-year marriage was in serious difficulties. They still loved each other but had got to the point where they seldom talked to each other. Both worked long hours and had arranged their schedules so that their nine-year-old could be taken to school and met by one of them. But this meant Jacqui started early and Jeremy finished late, and while their son had ample time with both parents, they had little time with each other. Both felt bitter and angry about the situation and blamed each other for the fact that their once-close relationship had deteriorated. The issue, they realized, was that, while they had lived together for two years before getting married, they'd then gone straight into having a child, giving them little time to spend with each other as a married couple. They both adored their son but acknowledged that they both wished they had waited before having him.

Key idea: Relationships are hard

Relationships require work and effort and attention. That might sound rather kill-joy, but the thing is that you get out what and as much as you put in.

A successful, and thus happy, secure and positive relationship demands certain skills – skills we don't, alas, learn in school but pick up from those around us. And, as I sadly see, many times we either don't learn those skills, or learn somewhat skewed versions that lead us into unhappy, insecure and highly negative relationships.

What happens in our childhood and our early relationships sets the scene for our adult ones. What we see between the adults that care for us gives us the model for how we expect relationships to go. And how those adults treat us gives us skills and embeds in us our expectations for ourselves – what we can do and what we are worth. On one extreme, you may have a child brought up seeing happy parents or carers who express their love for each other in open affection and who give that child unconditional love, with boundaries and rules. Such a child is likely to become an adult who has realistic expectations of themselves but who can give affection, make commitments, communicate their feelings and listen to the people they love, and be self-confident with good self-esteem. At the other extreme, you might have a child who sees parents or carers who are emotionally distant and possibly physically apart, who are unrealistic and inconsistent in what they offer and expect, who might be critical and judgemental and authoritarian without being authoritative. Such a child may become an adult who has low self-esteem and confidence and who, without realizing it, seeks out romantic partners in the same pattern – emotionally unavailable and unable to connect.

The importance of self-confidence

A lack of self-confidence can make it hard to establish a good relationship, and to demand from your partner and yourself that there be trust and truthfulness. One comment put the finger on why so many of our relationships can be difficult: 'I regret not pursuing a relationship because of my friend's comments about the person.' Many of the letters I receive paint a picture of people who trust other people's opinions above their own, or feel that they should give in to what others demand. 'I felt it wasn't working, but he insisted we were good together so I stayed with him even though I was unhappy.' Or:

> 'I married in the 1980s and we spent two happy years together. Then he began to go round to see his ex-wife and, while I understand they had to have contact as they had children, I felt hurt and betrayed and the only way I thought I could hurt him was to start divorce proceedings. He bombarded me with letters, roses, chocolates, but I was too stubborn. After we divorced we got back together, but my mother and sister were in the background "advising", so for a quiet life I listened to them and we lost contact. I later learned he had died, and since then I have carried feelings of guilt that I gave up too easily on our marriage and, when given a second chance, still listened to the wrong people.'

We all need approval

Children always want and need approval from their parents, and from the people they learn to trust and look up to. Being given approval is a vital building-block in establishing self-esteem and confidence. But there comes a point where what other people think of you becomes a trap. If you are told, as so many people are, that you are lovable and good and nice and admirable *when* you do the things the adults want, you will set their opinions up as the one thing you must earn. Even if what they are asking for is actually good for you, it still means you become addicted to other people's praise and opinions. So what happens when their belief in what is good for you diverts from yours, or when what they are asking for might actually be good for them but not you? Or when what they demand is inconsistent and confusing and changes from day to day? A lifetime of looking to other people for approval, for not trusting your own feelings and thoughts, can leave you open to abuse and misdirection.

Trust yourself

What can you do about this? For yourself, it's important to start to trust yourself. If you feel something is not working or not right in a relationship, listen to that voice. Qualms need to be addressed, no matter when or why. One reader of my agony page said:

> 'My sister is getting married next week and I know she's having second thoughts. This isn't just a case of last-minute nerves – they've lived together for two years. And during that time I know for certain he's had at least three affairs. She suspects it and that's why she's in two minds. But our mother is putting pressure on her not to "spoil things". She keeps going on about how much this has cost, the difficulty of cancelling arrangements and how it would make us look, and telling her she had doubts before her wedding and it's lasted 40 happy years. Dad, I must say, is saying nothing.'

It doesn't matter how difficult it might seem to confront a misgiving – it needs to be done. Separation and divorce may be the answer:

> 'I hung on for ten years with my first wife who was cold and demanding. I came from a happy home so I just thought that, once I'd made a choice, I had to tough it out and try and make things work. I finally saw a counsellor. My wife refused to come at first but then came to see what I'd been saying, she said. When I looked at it with clear eyes I began to realize that there were no upsides to our relationship, only downsides. I felt such a failure but we did get divorced. And what a relief it was. I've been with my second wife for 20 years now. I just shudder at the thought of what I could have missed.'

Divorce or counselling?

In some cases, opting for divorce to try and change things can leave you with even more regrets, especially if you have children. But whether you mend it or end it, what is always needed is a clear and honest appraisal of what you did, what you want and what you can do now. The problem is that so often when people seek help to address the difficulties in their relationships it's often too late. Anger and unhappiness have compounded over the years and this makes it hard to put people and relationships back together again. That's not to say it's impossible. The first stop when a relationship is experiencing difficulties should always be support of some kind – see the Appendix for suggestions. As one couple agreed:

> 'We had a really rough time when we'd been married for 11 years. On the one hand, we can say we wish we'd known before what we learned then by going to counselling. On the other, you can say at least we took the lessons and made our relationship better and stronger. I think we both regret things we said and did then. But here we are, 15 years on from that and grandparents and still in love.'

So what can you do to make your relationships as good as possible, and to let go of regrets from past mistakes?

Ten top tips for making your relationship work

1 **Get to know each other** – your pasts, your tastes, your little quirks. Tell each other stories about your past, fill each other in on what's going on now, and talk about your hopes for the future. Of course, partners shouldn't live in each other's pockets and we all need to keep some part of ourselves separate and private. But intimacy is what brings people together, and you can only be intimate with someone you really know.

2 **Set good habits** in the early days or bring them in now. Look at all the ways you showed your partner how much you loved them, and, if you've stopped doing them, bring them back. A hug, a kiss, a stroke on the arm, a cup of coffee – all say 'You matter to me' and all keep your relationship alive.

3 Once your relationship has settled into a comfortable routine, **keep reminding yourself and your partner what drew you together,** what attracted you to them, and the way you felt in the early days of your relationship. Focus on the positive aspects and keep them going.

4 **Make a point of doing something every day for your partner, and thank them out loud for anything they do that** pleases you. It can be something big or something small – every little thing helps.

5 Ensure that that every day – whatever other calls you have on your time – **you and your partner talk one to one** about what you've been doing and how you are feeling. It could be just to tell each other something that has happened to you that day. It could be to clear the air about something that has upset or hurt you.

6 **Regularly see your own friends** and do something that specially and specifically interests you to maintain your own individuality and social life. But share your thoughts, your ideas and your enthusiasms with your partner, so that you both keep in touch with this other side of yourselves and never keep secrets.

7 **Let yourself be spontaneous.** Relationships often go stale because it all becomes so predictable. If you're suddenly overcome with the urge to say 'I love you' or give them a smooch, don't hold back just because you've been married ten years or because you're standing in the queue at the supermarket. Do it, wherever or whenever. Let the moment pass and you'll get used to staying quiet, and soon both of you will get out of the habit.

8 **Make a big deal out of time together.** Even if money is tight and you're only spending the evening in eating sausage and mash and watching TV, make it an event. Take steps to ensure that you'll be on your own, dress up and splash yourself with cologne, turn the lights low and burn candles, and use the best china.

9 **Look after yourself!** Respect yourself and realize that you are worth while and deserve to love and be loved.

Case study: Jeremy and Jacqui (part 2)

Jeremy and Jacqui, having come to me with a marriage on the point of breaking up, realized that they had to do something to get back to the close and happy relationship they once had. The main issue was that both had focused on their son to the detriment of their own partnership. They had been model parents, with Jacqui taking a year off to care for him, then Jeremy taking over while she went back to work, then both of them sharing care until the boy went to school. This had produced a happy, secure and much-loved child, but the factor left out was their time together or focus on each other.

In therapy, they explored what had drawn them together, what they had liked doing as a couple and why they no longer did these activities. Jacqui resisted the idea of leaving their son with friends or family while they took some time off together, but eventually realized it was either that or see their problems continue. Evenings out as a couple developed into a weekend away, and then a week off on their own walking in France. It wasn't just the time away that made the difference – it was experiencing again the pleasure of being together and enjoying each other's company, and being able to translate that back into everyday life. Both realized that they needed to put as much effort into their own relationship as they did into being good parents, and that doing so paid off.

10 **Don't become addicted to praise.** It's lovely to have your abilities recognized and acknowledged and to say nice things about those around you. But it's important to avoid the trap of needing approval from others. After all, you can't please everyone all the time and some people not at all. The best way to help yourself and your family to do their best is to make self-recognition the gold standard. Listen to what other people say, but know your own strengths and weaknesses.

Over-praising our children

It's important, then, to release ourselves from the trap of needing praise from other people. It's equally important if we have children to help them never to fall into the same trap. What you can do for your children is make them responsible for their happiness, and to do that you make them responsible for their own praise. When you do give praise, make it descriptive.

In the old days, we tended to feel praising a child would 'spoil them' – they'd become complacent and arrogant. So now we do praise them, but we are in danger of going the other way, and *over*-praising, which can actually be as counterproductive as not praising them.

Never acknowledging effort or results so often leads to children feeling rejected and unappreciated. A child who proudly comes home with a 9 out of 10 for a school test and is told they should have got 10 out of 10 and to do better next time isn't spurred to try harder but becomes convinced that there is no point in trying. But today's parents seem to have replaced that with praising their child for doing the least little thing. Praise can raise a child's confidence and make them feel good about themselves – obviously a 'good thing' – and can also give them the incentive to earn your notice and your approval again. But over-praising can have the same effect as lack of praise. After all, if they can't quite see what it was they did that earned that praise, how can they know to repeat it? What may then happen is that the child, now afraid of not getting the usual praise, will draw back from even trying, in case this time they fail.

The value of descriptive praise

What is needed is what is known as 'descriptive praise'. We often think saying 'Well done, you!' is what is needed. And that's all very nice, but it doesn't work if it's given with a sour look, or if we follow it up with '...but why didn't you do it before I asked you to?' And it's no good if the child actually knows you don't mean it, or they don't really deserve it. So, praise is when we make a positive comment, in a warm and kind tone of voice, with a loving look, and it's genuine.

Descriptive praise is when you say clearly what it was they did that pleased you. Instead of 'Well done! What a good boy,' you say, 'You cleared up all your toys and put them away in the right boxes. The living room looks really tidy. Thank you!' The more precise your description, the better they know what you liked and why you are pleased. The child then knows that they can do this task and can repeat it another time and earn more praise. It feels a bit odd to do this at first and can take some practice. But when you see how effective it is you'll realize it's worth doing.

And while you are about it, use descriptive praise with your partner, too. It works with adults as much as with children!

Here are some good phases to use:

- ▶ 'Thank you for that. You... and then you... That was really helpful/kind/useful.'

- ▶ 'You worked really hard to do that – well done!'

- ▶ 'You kept on and didn't give up.'

- ▶ 'You showed kindness – thank you!'

- ▶ 'Are you pleased with yourself? You should be!'

- ▶ 'Are you proud of what you did? You should be!'

- ▶ 'I like it when you...'

- ▶ 'I like the way you...'

- ▶ 'I thought it was really good when you...'

- 'I could see you were trying hard.'
- 'Look at how you...'
- 'I can trust you to... because you...'

Remember this: Points to consider

- Love, sex and relationships are the major causes of problems and regrets in our lives and deserve our constant attention.

- Self-confidence is an essential part of making and keeping relationships.

- Even the best relationships can be hard work. You will need all your insight and skill to keep them happy and successful.

- Knowing when and how to praise is an important part of a relationship, whether it's with a child or an adult.

Helping children, and helping yourself, to appreciate and be pleased with your own efforts and abilities teaches a reliance, not on other people's approval or opinions, but on your own. It means that when you know something is wrong you can take steps to change it. And when you know it is right you can resist other people's attempts to make you back down.

Try it now: Dinnertime game

A good way of learning and reinforcing this ability to pay attention to your own abilities and trust yourself is a game to play over the evening meal table – it's called 'Three Things'. You might play it on your own, with a partner or with your family – even very young children. Ask everyone to consider and explain:

* 'one thing I did today that I'm pleased about'
* 'one thing today that I would have liked to have been different'
* 'one thing I'd like to do tomorrow'.

One thing I did today that I'm pleased about

This can be something small and trivial, or immense and important. It can be complete or the start of something we'll go back to later. It can be private or something lots of people saw and know about. The key is for the person speaking to reflect on their own triumph – something they and maybe no one else realizes was important to them and meant something, and about which they are pleased. They key is for them to pat themselves on the back about it.

One thing today that I would have liked to have been different

This allows the person to reflect on something they would have liked to have done better or had someone else do better for them. It can allow the person involved to think about failing. We should all learn how to fail. Children need to get the message from us that they should feel good about being wrong, and we should reinforce the message to ourselves, too. That's because failing is the best way of learning a lesson. If you get it wrong and messed up this time, that's the way to learn how to do it differently next time. You don't succeed by always succeeding because sooner or later you are going to come up against something you can't do first time, and how do you know how to be resilient and try again, if you haven't had to do it? Failing is no big deal, as long as we learn from it – and then it is a big deal that we be allowed to fail in order to learn.

One thing I'd like to do tomorrow

This allows plans to be made so that you can continue to trust your own decisions and opinions and to make a stab at overcoming the mistakes of today.

There are no right or wrongs in this game, and it's important for everyone to listen to and accept what other people are choosing as their triumphs and failings. It's about learning to trust yourself, which is an important step to making good relationships, or dealing with ones that have gone bad.

Top tips for improving relationships

▶ **Demand the best.** So often we settle for second best. We accept or stay in a relationship because we don't want to be alone or, as we see it, suffer the stigma of being 'on the shelf'. So we say yes to being with someone who doesn't make us feel cherished and cared for, who is careless about our needs or feelings, or who is maybe even downright abusive. At the heart of the decision to be there and stay there may be an unconscious assumption that we deserve this – that we can't do any better, that this is what relationships are all about and we don't deserve better. But we do. We'd take shoddy goods back to the shop… or we certainly should! So do the same with a shoddy relationship – send it back.

▶ **Do as you would…** If you want to be treated well, one strategy is to 'model' the behaviour you would like. Be kind, respectful, loving, decent, honest and caring, and the chances are the other person will respond in kind. You show how it's done and you set the scene. But also remind yourself of the standards you expect in a mutually caring relationship and, if it isn't reciprocated, either sort this out (see later) or remove yourself.

▶ **Communicate, communicate, communicate**. Relationships simply don't work unless you communicate. And communication is two-way – you have to listen as much as you express your own thoughts and feelings. We can't read minds, so you can't expect your partner to know what you anticipate, want or need, nor can you assume that you know what is going on in their minds. Gill emailed me through my agony page to say:

> *'Year after year I'd get fed up and disappointed because my husband gave me lousy presents and decided Valentine's Day was for idiots. I read what you said about not giving hints or expecting him to know what you wanted and letting him know clearly. So I told him I'd really like it if he'd pay attention when I said I like something, and if he took on board that I'd love a Valentine's card. Well… you were right! I've had a Christmas, a birthday and a Valentine's Day since I did that and for each one he's been wonderful! And I'm sure he'll go on now he's "got it"… and because I gave him such a reception to give him a good incentive! Thank you, Suzie!'*

▶ **Don't put your head in the sand.** It's easy to get the idea that, once you have a settled relationship, you can ride off into the sunset for your 'happily ever after'. In fact, relationships are dynamic and change and grow constantly. This means that, just because all is going swimmingly at first, you can't get complacent. And when things do begin to go wrong, turning a blind eye and hoping things will go back to running smoothly on their own is a mistake. Don't put your head in the sand about rows, misunderstanding and resentments. When a problem raises its ugly head, do something about it as soon as possible.

▶ **Watch for crunch points.** There are certain points in any relationship where you will come under pressure. We call them crunch or pinch points. These are the times when your situation or circumstances change – such as when you go from the honeymoon period to ordinary life, when you have a child, when you change a job, when you move house, when your children start or change school, when they become teenagers, and so on. Change of any sort is hard, even when it's a positive change or one we've anticipated. Knowing that it's normal to struggle at such times makes it easier to manage.

▶ **Make a date.** Relationships can go stale because a couple get out of the habit of spending special time together. It can be because free time is spent with the kids or catching up on housework or attending to friends and family who shout the loudest. The trick is to schedule time alone as a couple the way you'd make a date when first going out, or setting aside time in the diary for important engagements. Time together is important, so make dates. Once a week organize a night out or a special night in together; once a month a day out together; once every six months a weekend away together. Keep to the schedule and you won't grow apart.

▶ **Be honest and clear.** Misunderstandings and resentments can build up when you're not honest and clear. When asked, we often grit our teeth and say we're fine when in fact we're angry, resentful or frustrated. It's so much better to take a deep breath and say: 'Well, no, actually, I'm really upset because…' We tend to keep quiet because we think saying what we think or feel will cause conflict. Really, far worse conflict happens when we suppress our feelings and then can't help but let them burst out, multiplied by being kept under wraps. It also helps to be specific about what has upset us. The magic formula is to say:

▷ 'When...

▷ I feel...

▷ because...

▷ What I would like is...'

▶ **Share work and play.** Relationships can seem to be best when all your time together is spent enjoying yourself – such as when you have a long-distance relationship and only see each other at weekends. Or when one of you does all the work for the family, leaving the other to just be there for party time. Alternatively, in a busy life you can find yourself on a treadmill of having to do essential jobs on your evenings and weekends, with no time to share rest and relaxation. Neither lifestyle does a relationship any favours. The best way to share your lives, to get to know each other, to enjoy time together and foster respect is to share both aspects equally.

▶ **Understand your feelings.** Sometimes a storm seems to come out of nowhere and we find ourselves furious with a partner – out of all proportion to the offence, perhaps, or even seemingly for no reason at all. What we often miss is that negative feelings can be echoes from the past, not reactions to the present. Somebody does something, says something, that reminds you of a past event or slight. Before you know it, you're reacting to that unresolved problem in addition to the present situation – pain or anger doubled, as it were.

▶ Feelings, whether of sadness, anger or resentment or whatever, are an expression of need. Maybe we need to be noticed, to be soothed, to be respected. Our need drives our feelings, which then drive our behaviour – whether that is to explode with rage or dissolve into tears. Instead of reaching for the baseball bat or the tissues, the best thing we can do when overtaken by emotions is to ask ourselves: 'What's my need? What's my feeling? And what might be about to be my behaviour?' Thinking about these things can often help you put your finger on what you need and why... and that can lead to your asking for a better response than you might have got by just reacting.

▶ **Resolve arguments and solve problems**. It's a cliché but nonetheless true that you shouldn't go to bed on an argument. The point is that, if you have a problem and simply sweep it under the carpet, it doesn't go away. It festers and is often joined by more swept-away and hidden issues, building up to a toxic heap of unhappiness. And this, sooner or later, will explode into something of epic proportions. It's difficult to resolve a situation that may by then have so many parts that it's downright impossible to work out what it's all about. The message here is that, each time you have an argument or a problem, focus on it and resolve it as soon as possible. It's relatively easy to deal with 'I'm upset because I felt you didn't appreciate how much I wanted to spend time with you yesterday.' If you leave it until five years of 'And another thing…' have built up, it can be extremely hard to untangle.

▶ **Accept change**. Change occurs. Change is always hard, but it's a fact of life and the best relationships happen when the couple and the family recognize that you have to go with the flow and adapt. Each pinch point may be hard to get through but can herald new adventures and new developments. Having the ability to maybe mourn your losses – yes, it's a shame the honeymoon can't go on – means you can also see the upside in what comes next – yes, once you really know each other trust grows and grows.

▶ **Keep the love alive and revisit good times**. We do develop and move on, but sometimes it helps to look back on the things we first valued in a relationship, and revisit those times. This can be as simple as saying 'Do you remember when…? Let's go there, do that again for old time's sake!' to mounting a full-scale re-enactment of early days. Making an effort to recall what it was that brought you together can revitalize the feelings you had then.

▶ **Don't tell even 'white' lies**. Whatever its colour, a lie is a lie and it corrodes trust, destroys confidence and frequently is at the root of massive regret. Lying is exhausting and stressful. It's hard to keep a lie going – you tend to have to embellish and enlarge. Even when not discovered, lies poison relationships. When they do come to light, it's not only the specific lie that hurts but the fact that you told one. Don't confuse lying with being tactful – the latter may require you to be kind and say nothing. Lying, whatever your excuse, is always self-serving and harmful to everyone concerned.

▶ **Ask for help**. All relationships can go through sticky patches. Very rarely will those be resolved by simply ignoring the trouble and forging on. Sometimes you can put yourself back on track by some of the strategies we've already discussed. But sometimes you need some professional help. There is no shame in asking for it – the reason why the sort of help offered by organizations such as Relate or Family Lives exists is because it's so common to need it! Sources of help can be found in the Appendix – do use it.

▶ **Recognize that life's too short...** ...to sweat the small things. If you have serious problems, then take the time and effort and ask for help to resolve them. But cultivate an attitude that lets trivial issues wash off your back – there are more important things in life than worrying about those dust bunnies under your bed.

'No road is long with good company.'

Turkish proverb

Your Action Plan: Step 6 – learn from your regrets

Step 6 of the Action Plan is to take lessons from our regrets – to make use of them to learn something, in order to move on with a life of fewer regrets. That doesn't mean having a life of no regrets – that's being unrealistic. But it does mean taking the advice of the Serenity Prayer – learning what you can't change and accepting it and learning what you can change and doing it.

Having fewer regrets often means facing problems squarely instead of avoiding them. Rather than pushing problems behind us, we need to look for solutions and apply them instead of running away, which is what most often leads to regrets. By facing issues we can often learn to seize the day and live in the moment instead of always looking either back or forward, dwelling on regrets or creating new ones. Key notes may include:

▶ **Regret serves a function.** A bit like pain, regret is a warning. Pain tells you not to lean on the hot stove, and regret tells you that you could have done something differently. Instead of getting mired in disappointment and despair, what regret should do is act as a spur to make a different decision next time.

▶ **You can learn about yourself.** One function of regret may be to let you follow what Alexander Pope said: 'Know then thyself, presume not God to scan; / The proper study of Mankind is Man.' If aspects of your past cause you pain or frustration or sadness, it can be an incentive to understand why you do things, why you feel things, why you might follow certain patterns and accept certain limitations. My books *Be More Assertive* and *How to Have a Happy Family Life* can give you many clues and much support in pursuing personal development and better relationships.

▶ **You should deal with your regrets.** Dwelling on regrets but not really dealing with them can leave them to fester. Taking the bull by the horns and drawing up a plan to address your regrets can move you on.

▶ **You are able to motivate yourself.** Suppressing regrets can mean you continue in the same vein, which places you in the danger zone open to new ones. Recognizing and looking at regrets can motivate you to address the ones in the past, and make sure you don't fall into the same trap in the future.

▶ **You can do something.** What's the worst that can happen? Often we think it's taking a risk and crashing and burning. In fact, I'd suggest that the worst thing is never taking a chance – you may stay safe but you'll never achieve anything. Recognizing regrets can encourage you to do something – anything! You may not succeed and get it right every time, but you'll do better in the long run than if you do nothing.

▶ **Seize the day.** Looking backwards all the time can be stultifying. It may help to consider regrets, but you shouldn't let that fix you in a state of mind that prioritizes looking back. Looking forwards can be healthy but not if it prevents you recognizing that it's OK to fail and learn from that failure. But one important message we need to take on board is to seize the day. A mindset we can fall into when children or teenagers is always looking forward to being bigger or growing up. As adults we might focus all the time on next year's holiday or when we get a promotion or when we lose weight... Sometimes, however, we need to be in the present – to enjoy what we have now.

Focus points

✳ Relationships are at the centre of most people's lives, so they should be at the centre of our consideration at all times.

✳ Relationships do not come easily or without effort. They require self-confidence to get them and then awareness and hard work to keep them.

✳ Always trust yourself and listen to yourself, and then address any relationship qualms you might have.

✳ Use this chapter's Action Plan and the ten top tips to make your relationship work as a maintenance manual for your own relationships.

✳ Have an honest look at how you give, and receive, praise. Knowing how and when to give praise is a key issue in any relationship.

✳ Demand the best you can get if you are to avoid the regrets that settling for an easy second best can bring. 'Do unto others...' is the way to get the best for you. Good relationships are reciprocal and, if you don't give, you don't get.

✳ Change is a part of life, so learn to go with the flow and to adapt when it's necessary.

✳ Get to know someone properly before moving on to a friendship, a relationship or a marriage. This will avoid having to deal with a 'toxic' situation later on.

✳ Communicate, communicate, communicate!

Next step

The next chapter, on health, looks at how failure to look after ourselves and our families properly can lead to future regret, and discusses what's important in getting or recovering a healthy lifestyle.

8

'I wish I had made my body a temple!'

In this chapter you will learn:

- ▶ *Why you might have the body and health you have now, and what might have brought them about*
- ▶ *How you might regret what might have been bad choices earlier, and how you can begin to correct and improve things*
- ▶ *How to see what's important in recovering or getting a healthy lifestyle, and how to prioritize your efforts*
- ▶ *The ten steps you can take towards a better lifestyle for you and your family*
- ▶ *How to use the Action Plan to find out how you can cherish and accept yourself.*

Healthy living

Serious regrets can gather around the way we treat our bodies as we get older. We may look back as we struggle with our health and fitness and wish we'd kept up certain pastimes or made sensible eating or regular exercise a priority. In previous generations we could at least enjoy the free ticket that was childhood and adolescence. Most young people were fit and healthy simply by virtue of being young and running about, and eating the good diet prescribed by their parents and school. The rot might set in when they left school and became independent and dropped exercise and took up bad eating and drinking habits. Nowadays, with a terrifying rise in childhood obesity and such conditions as diabetes, it seems that even being young no longer protects you – health and fitness are issues we need to actively pursue at all times in our lives.

Many of my questionnaire respondents had specific regrets about the way they had looked after themselves and the results that this has had. Several said their regret was 'taking up smoking!' One said that their regret was:

> 'giving up sport at university. I was seriously good at school, I've always loved sport but I didn't want to look like a jock to my new cool friends. They wouldn't have minded, of course.'

All recognized that such decisions had an inevitable effect on their health. One man said:

> 'I drank too much – far too much. I was a drunk, truth be told. In my own experience, quitting drinking was very difficult, and the only thing that made it possible was that the pain of change was less than the pain of staying the same. And because I finally faced up to the fact that, if I didn't quit, I'd have so many regrets they'd sink me.'

The problem is that, while as adults we may know what is good for us, our choices about health, healthy eating and exercise may not reflect that knowledge. The main problem can be that so many other issues dictate what we do and those can override our good sense.

> 'If we could give every individual the right amount of nourishment and exercise, not too little and not too much, we would have found the safest way to health.'
>
> Hippocrates

Appearance may initially be the spur to behaviour, so looking cool or being like our friends is likely to take precedence over other considerations. Avoiding obesity may be an excellent goal but, for most, weight is about looking good rather than being healthy. 'I regret my obsession with weight, especially when younger' and 'I wish I had not worried so much about my weight and looks as an adolescent. I spent so much times thinking about whether I looked "right" when really I should have relished my individuality' were typical comments. The reality is that what you look like may not always reflect what is going on in your heart, arteries, liver and lungs.

Why do we so often make such bad choices? As children we may have little choice – we do as we are led by our parents, or we align ourselves with the people we'd like to blend in with or copy, our peer group. A letter to my agony page described just such a situation:

> 'My daughter had no food fads at all when she was little – she loved fresh fruit and vegetables and would eat carrot sticks as a treat. Then she started school and all of a sudden she wouldn't eat this, wouldn't eat that and became so fussy. She's now eight and her brother is six and some nights I'm making four different meals for me, both children and my husband if he's late home. It's driving me crazy. And it's also expensive. You think buying frozen economy fish fingers, pizza and burgers would be cheap, but it seems to add up and now I'm worried what's really in them.'

But even when we mature we can follow the patterns laid down in our childhood. We might now seem to have a global obsession with cookery shows on TV and cookery books are on all the bestselling lists, but the reality is that we buy more fast food and pre-prepared dishes than ever before.

Even if we were brought up on home-cooked and healthy food, the chances are that with our busy schedules the first thing that often goes is meals round a table together and that can mean an inevitable slide into quick and easy convenience food.

Eating well

READ THE LABELS

If you buy food that comes in a packet, jar or carton, read the list of ingredients and note the amount of sugar, salt and fat. Be aware that these are often quoted as 'per 100 grams' when the container is larger than that. The yoghurt that you thought was only 63 calories is actually 157.5 because you eat the whole 250-gram pot. A serving of frankfurters or a quarter-pounder with medium fries and a medium coke gives you half your calories for a day.

Even apparently 'healthy' food such as pasta or chicken dishes can contain more fats, sugars and salt than would be in a similar home-cooked dish. Pre-prepared food often contains ingredients that give it 'mouth feel' – so it feels creamy and satisfying – and extra flavourings such as salt to tickle your taste buds. In fact, they usually contain far more salt, fat or sugar than you expect, or ingredients that you might not normally associate with that particular food. Would you expect milk in Chinese food, or salt in bread and cereals? It's there, so it adds to your overall intake.

Adults shouldn't eat more than 6 grams – a teaspoon – of salt a day and children should have less. And labels may conceal salt by calling it sodium chloride. Multiply by 2.5 and you get the amount of salt it contains. Excess salt contributes to high blood pressure leading to heart attacks and stroke – and it doesn't do your weight any good, either, because salty foods are often high in fat.

MAKE MEALS FROM SCRATCH

Sadly, only a small minority of families now cook meals from scratch, hardly any never use ready meals and the vast majority admit to using pre-prepared meals not just sometimes but regularly – if not all the time. And this is exactly why we have several problems rife in our society at present. We're overweight, we're unfit and in many homes the people living there hardly talk together and live parallel lives. Make a meal from scratch and you get several benefits. You can be aware of, and control, the amount of salt, sugar and fat you put in it – you only use what is appropriate. It will be cost-efficient, too – putting together a ragu sauce for pasta takes not much longer than microwaving or heating one from a jar and costs less. It is also fun – everyone who is about to eat it can join in preparing it so you're far less likely to get complaints. And, of course, both the cooking and the eating together are social activities that build bonds and entertain you.

> 'A bear, however hard he tries, grows tubby without exercise.'
> A.A. Milne, *Winnie-the-Pooh*

Move it!

Two American presidents seemed to have the right idea about exercise. Thomas Jefferson said, 'Leave all the afternoon for exercise and recreation, which are as necessary as reading. I will rather say more necessary because health is worth more than learning,' while John F. Kennedy said. 'Physical fitness is not only one of the most important keys to a healthy body, it is the basis of dynamic and creative intellectual activity.' So why is it so hard to continue the instinct we have as young children to run around and stay fit? Whatever the reason, it's a tendency we need to fight. The sad part is that it doesn't need to take either time or money to retain basic fitness. The best scenario might be to cycle instead of drive, to run instead of watching TV, to go to a gym or to swim regularly. But if that seems too pricey or you feel you can't make time in your busy life, you could make some easy changes in everyday routines that make a difference:

▸ Never take lifts, up or down.

▸ Get off the bus or train a stop early on every trip or park your car some distance away from your destination.

- If your journey is less than 3 kilometres (2 miles), walk. One mile should take you 20 minutes. Make the time.

- When working or studying, regularly get up from the table or desk for a few minutes' activity – it apparently 'resets' your body, getting all systems working instead of vegetating.

- Instead of inactive weekend pastimes, think of creating bonds and enjoying time together doing something energetic – walking, cycling, throwing a Frisbee, playing tennis or squash or football or hockey or…

Key idea: *Mens sana in corpore sano*

We tend to see fitness as something extra, something only elite sportspeople or people on a diet possess, but having the habit of regular exercise makes us much happier as well as much healthier. Fitness boosts self-esteem and confidence, and doesn't have to cost the earth. A gym membership would actually pay off in the way it improves your life, but, if that seems a bit excessive, running or walking can give you the same benefits for less. Whatever the excuses, anyone can make time in their schedule to fit in a run during their lunchtime, getting up half an hour early to walk to work or school, and making one of your days off the time you do something energetic as a family.

Drinking...

'Drink no longer water, but use a little wine for thy stomach's sake and thine often infirmities' is one of the better-known biblical exhortations, and it's often used to mean 'Don't be prissy – booze is good for you.' And we tend to pay more attention to the suggestion that a glass of red wine a day improves heart health than the evidence that shows that even moderate alcohol consumption can increase blood pressure, lead to heart problems and stroke, damage the liver and pancreas, and increase your risk of suffering cancer of the mouth, throat, liver and breast. In any case, St Paul (who gave the advice) was talking at a time when you couldn't guarantee the quality of the water available to drink – wine might be a better option than the soup of bacteria and protozoa probably found in most water sources and that often led to illness and diseases – 'thine often infirmities'. And wine in those days was also probably a lot weaker than ours.

There is still a lot of debate about this subject, but safe drinking is usually agreed to be no more than 14 units a week for women and 21 for men, taken over several nights but not every night. Most bottles will now tell you their strength – from 3 to 8 per cent alcohol in light beers with most around 5 to 6, and up to 14 or 14½ per cent for a bottle of wine. But the important figure you need to understand is the unit per glass. One unit – to go towards that 14 or 21 in a week – is not the same as a drink. A large glass of wine, for instance, can amount to three or even four units, which should be your limit for a night. The healthiest pattern to follow is that you never drink every day, and you very, very rarely if ever exceed your weekly limit. Holidays and feast days may throw you off schedule but, if they do, compensate with a corresponding period alcohol free. If you won't think of your heart, your organs and your brain, think about your waistline – all benefit profoundly from you being careful about your alcohol intake.

...and smoking

We shouldn't be too puritanical about drinking, which, after all, is a great pleasure. It's the amount and the frequency that matter, and you can weigh up the downsides of possibly raising your risk of suffering some conditions with even a small amount of regular alcohol against the benefits from that pleasure. What you cannot do under any circumstances is make any case for even the smallest amount of smoking. We've all heard the justifications – 'It's relaxing', 'It's my only treat', 'It's something just for me.' None of these stack up against the fact that smoking is a killer. Nicotine is also probably the most addictive substance we ingest, and that's really what is going on. It's not a pleasure, it's not a treat – if you smoke, you're addicted, and that's that.

All the justifications are to cover up the fact that smoking is a really hard thing to stop. The actual discomfort can be overcome in a relatively short time – you'll stop having physical cravings in a few days to a week. What you may find, however, is that the habit of reaching for a cigarette in certain circumstances and at certain times takes much longer to conquer. And because we often take up smoking to overcome social awkwardness, shyness, lack of self-confidence or low self-esteem, we may well find these unexpectedly returning, and with some force. It's not easy to give up. But if, like so many people, you look at your physical health and your bank balance and deeply regret starting, you're going to regret even more not stopping if you don't.

A few facts about smoking

- Every year approximately 120,000 smokers in the UK die as a consequence of their smoking.
- Half of all regular smokers will eventually be killed by their habit.
- Smoking causes approximately 80 per cent of all deaths from lung cancer and bronchitis. Non-smokers rarely get lung cancer – those who do tend to be people who live with smokers.
- Smoking increases your risk of having a heart attack by two to three times that of a non-smoker
- More than 17,000 children in the UK are admitted to hospital every year because of the effects of passive smoking.

Case study: Jenny

'I knew I should give up smoking. That was my deepest regret, starting. But it was so hard – I tried a couple of times and found I just got so ratty that my husband was driven to tell me to go back to get me off his back. One day I looked in the mirror and saw all these lines on my face and a friend laughed and said 'Oh, yeah – smoker's face!' That was it. I saw my doctor and got some help and I've been off a year. I can't believe how much money I've saved!'

What's important?

If building exercise and healthy eating into your schedule sounds time consuming, perhaps it's time to consider your priorities. It's going to blow a hole in your schedule when you start to suffer the ill health that comes with a sedentary lifestyle and an unwise diet. And being unhealthy can be expensive, too, in lost work days or early redundancy or unplanned and premature retirement.

Try it now: Change your and your family's lifestyle

For the next week, get everyone in the family to keep a strict diary of everything you do with your time:

1 Note exactly what you do from hour to hour – your morning routine, your commute to work or school/college, what you do at work and in your break times, your commute home, your shopping, what meals you prepare and how, what you and your family or partner do in the evenings and at weekends – everything.
2 Note also points of conflict – when you argue and why.
3 Once you all have a full picture of your and your family's day, hold an ideas-storming session (see Chapter 2), to see how you might benefit by changing your routines.

Here are some of the things people I've helped said after carrying out this exercise:

> 'Every evening it seemed we'd have a row as soon as I got home that meant dinner was late and somebody was up in their room sulking. We tried two things. One was that I had ten minutes of "do not talk to me" time when I went up, had a shower, changed and listened to two tracks on my iPod. Then I'd come down in a relaxed mood ready to give the family all my attention and listen to them. Magic! Hardly any rows now because I was ready for them. Second, we started cooking the evening meal together. It meant we could talk as we did it and everyone was in the kitchen having a good time. When we first did it my son would be upstairs on his PlayStation as usual. After a week he realized he was missing out. The amount of time he's spending on that thing has dropped – a lot.' (Paul)

> 'I'd been saying going to a gym was too expensive and we didn't have the time. Then I looked at the time we spent just slumped watching the box and Geoff added up the

amount he was spending on fags. He cut down, we met there after work and the end result was actually you didn't feel as if we'd lost any time from our evening. But we both lost a stone and felt better.' (Marie)

'We never seemed to eat together because our two children had so many after-school activities and we were either driving them here and there, or doing our own. And that meant ready meals or takeaways most of the time. It was breaking the bank, so we decided to cut down on a few activities but do something together – we started going out for a bike ride once a week. And we insisted on two meals a weekday night together, and one on weekends. And then we found that, instead of all of us being on the mobile or laptop or watching TV in separate rooms, we were hanging around together because… well, we liked it. And we don't have nearly as many arguments as we used to – stuff gets sorted in the kitchen or round the table.' (Lee)

Body art

A few respondents mentioned regretting having had tattoos and piercings when they were younger. Barry said:

'I was in the Navy and had a few done. When I came out and wanted to join the police it was a problem and now I'm a respectable teacher I really regret it. Some of the lads have seen them and think they're cool, but it's not something I can show at parents' night.'

And Ana said:

'I had a whole slew of piercings done when I was a teenager and in my twenties – not just face but all over my body. I was so embarrassed when I saw the midwife in my first pregnancy!'

Of course, you may have perfectly good reasons for getting tattoos or pierced. Terri said:

'The one thing I've never regretted, in 15 years, is getting a tattoo of a climbing rose on my back and shoulder. It cost me more than I could afford at the time, took ages and was

quite painful at times. But I relished getting it and having it. Why? Because I was anorexic as a teenager. I spent my whole twenties struggling with the condition. Falling in love at thirty and then marrying and wanting children gave me the incentive to change. I began the tattoo on my 35th birthday, to celebrate giving birth. My teenage daughter thinks it's a hoot. It was my way of reclaiming my body and loving it by adorning it. It was my way of promising not to go back.'

Of course, the rule should be that you need to think carefully before doing anything irrevocable. Tattoos can be removed, but still leave scars. Piercings can simply be left out and are less noticeable – but they still never heal over. The reality is that what was regarded as edgy and rebellious 20 years ago is today fairly mainstream. In a generation or so, many a grandparent will still have a design on their lower back or shoulder and it will be hardly worth remarking upon. But it's still something worth considering carefully and, if it's too late, at least have the discussion with the next generation – sharing your experience may help them think twice.

Body changes

And what about Botox, cosmetic surgery or other forms of body changes?

'I was feeling so depressed about the way my forehead was showing wrinkles so I had Botox. It worked fine but the weird thing was that, after a few weeks of feeling really good about it, I went back to being depressed. I had two courses and then I saw my GP about my depression and she said it was probably the Botox itself that wasn't helping. I stopped using it, took her advice to talk to someone about how I was feeling and things did improve.'

Cosmetic surgery can limit our ability to show emotion. Recent research has showed that, if you can't show emotion, you will have difficulty communicating with others. They can't read your emotions if they aren't reflected in your face and this leads to misunderstandings. But more important is the fact that this also has a significant effect on you: interfere with your ability to show emotions and you will soon feel dejected.

Any permanent alteration to your body does have to be taken seriously, and has to be considered in all lights. Tammy said:

> *'I had my ears pinned back when I was a teenager – I'd had years of being teased about them. I can't tell you the difference it made to me. So then, when I was old enough to pay for it myself, I had breast enhancement and a nose job, even though my parents and my boyfriend said my nose was perfectly fine before. It made a real difference to my self-confidence. Recently, I saw the same surgeon to ask about having my lips and cheeks done and he said I should see a counsellor first. I think that's unnecessary.'*

The problem is that, while we may feel secure and happy when we think our body is 'right', and depressed and insecure when we think it is 'wrong', often what is more important is our state of mind. The more resilient and secure you feel about yourself, the less important is your actual appearance. To a certain extent, we can lift our own mood and bring ourselves self-confidence by optimizing our health, our fitness and, thus, how we look. However, making your body a temple means attending to simple health issues, not going to extremes so that you can have a body like a celebrity's. You know they do that by unhealthy diet, unrealistic exercise and surgery, don't you? Oh – and digital manipulation.

Remember this: Points to consider

▶ You may have made bad earlier choices about your lifestyle, or had no choice at all. But there is always time to realize that something needs to be done and to take action.

▶ You are likely to be more successful if you deal with the really important things first by prioritizing your efforts.

▶ Think long and hard, and take professional advice if you are unsure, before trying the apparently easy route of undertaking things like crash diets, cosmetic surgery, Botox or body art.

▶ Try to see the distinction between how you 'feel' about yourself and how you actually are.

Ten easy steps to fitness

1 **Get enough rest.** You need several hours of deep sleep every night to refresh you, but you don't always need to sleep for seven or eight hours. What you do need to do is rest. Too many after-midnight stop-outs and your skin, your hair, your weight and your ability to make decisions go west. Aim to go to bed in time for you to be there for seven or eight hours a night, most nights.

2 **Eat fresh food, during meals you and your family have prepared together.** Have fish twice a week and fresh veg or salad at every meal.

3 You *don't* have to walk around with a little plastic bottle all the time but do **make sure you drink enough water**. It can be in the form of coffee (make it mostly decaff) or tea. Don't drink too much fruit juice, however – it's full of calories and bad for your teeth.

4 **Drink alcohol moderately** – don't spoil a good thing.

5 **Don't smoke.** At all. Period. And talking of periods, did you know smoking can make them more irregular and painful? They can bring on your menopause early, too, giving you a higher risk of developing conditions such as osteoporosis. Men don't get off scot-free, either. Smoking increases your likelihood of suffering erectile dysfunction.

6 **De-stress, regularly.** Schedule rest and relaxation moments – for whole hours, days and weekends. But forget so-called 'detox' diets, which are an unnecessary hype. Your liver detoxes you. It doesn't need help in the form of a diet, although it does need you to drink only moderately and smoke not at all.

7 **If you don't feel well, don't put on a brave face.** Obviously, leave your doctor alone if you have a cold, because they can't give you any treatments that will deal with a virus anyway, and it will cure itself in three to four days. But don't put off asking for advice for illnesses you suspect or know need attention.

8 **Accept all your GP surgery's invitations to screening and health checks.** Take the opportunity to see health as something positive, not just the absence of ill health, and something we can invest in and affect.

9 **Go for a healthy weight your body accepts as correct** and you can maintain it with a reasonable regime of good eating and enjoyable exercise. Avoid the ridiculous pursuit of the size 0 'ideal' that will have you yo-yo-ing and feeling miserable.

10 If you want to adorn yourself with tattoos and piercings, fine. Make sure, however, that you get them from registered practitioners and plan ahead on what they will look like and how you will feel about them in 20 years. And consider your reasons – many of which can be perfectly good.

Your Action Plan: Step 7 – cherish yourself

Step 7 of your Action Plan is to look at ways of looking after and cherishing yourself. If you love and accept yourself and see the positives in your life instead of always dwelling on the negatives, you are far more likely to make the changes that ensure that your life will be lived with fewer regrets. Try to do the following:

▶ **Accept yourself – body and soul.** We so often spend useless time, effort and regrets on what we look like – we obsess that we're too fat, too skinny, too muscled, not muscled enough. The curious thing is that some of the most admired people have 'blemishes', as we might think of them if we were them. Singer Jennifer Lopez has a big butt, actress Brooke Shields has thick eyebrows, actress and singer Barbra Streisand has a big nose. None of them did what actress Jennifer Gray, the star of *Dirty Dancing*, did, which was have plastic surgery to 'correct' the shape of her nose. In doing so, she made herself bland and anonymous-looking, removed the character from her face and nearly wrecked her career. In contrast, J-Lo made a feature of her figure; the other two simply made it clear you that you should take them or leave them. I have a friend who had big pop eyes but who made a point of wearing dramatic, Cleopatra-style makeup that emphasized them and made you see them as beautiful. All of these people could see the beauty in themselves and, in doing so, imposed their vision on other people.

▶ **Choose what you do with your time.** We so often spend the majority of our time looking after everyone but ourselves. Parents of both sexes, but particularly mothers, are prone to this, and women as a whole tend to let everyone else push by and go first. 'I'd love to have coffee with you but I've got to collect Johnny from his friends / make dinner / do the laundry…' So cherishing yourself is sometimes about making decisions about your time to do the best for you. Everyone in your family and friendship group deserves to have their needs met – but so do you.

▶ **Do what you want to do.** None of us wants to be selfish – but sometimes being selfish means looking after yourself, and that's important. You need, sometimes, to go with what is important to you, even if those around you either don't understand or find it hard to be supportive. You want to run a marathon? Don't listen to the naysayers – do it. You want to go back to college? Listen to what other people say, but marshal your arguments and carry the day. Would you like to join an evening class even though it means that your family have to look after themselves one night a week? It doesn't even need thinking about – of course you should!

▶ **Treat yourself.** This might mean knowing when it's OK to splurge on a new pair of jeans. It may also mean knowing when it's the right time to insist on half an hour reading a book or listening to music and when to have that hot bath with a glass of something when no one is allowed to interrupt you. Even a cup of coffee at the right time is a treat – whatever makes you feel relaxed, cherished and cared for.

▶ **Find your talent.** Maybe from your past you keep hearing a voice that tells you that you're useless and worthless and will never amount to much. Maybe you do feel there's nothing you excel at. The truth is that we all have talents – multiple abilities in which we can be competent and expert. Sometimes it just needs us to find one thing that we do well to break the dam and let us discover more. So find your talent. What do you do well? Maybe your cupcakes always get raves, or you can sew a mean seam. Or maybe you're a 'cat-caller' – someone cats always run towards and brush up against. Or you can soothe babies or put together a stylish outfit. Find your talent, pat yourself on the back for being so capable – then go out and find more talents.

▶ **Appreciate what is around you.** Sometimes cherishing yourself begins with cherishing what is around you. Notice the sunsets, glory in the autumn colours or spring flowers, enjoy the simple pleasure of a warm day or an honest-to-goodness thunderstorm. Look up when you walk down a crowded city street – often the top storeys of those formidable, dirty buildings have amazing embellishments.

▶ **Count your blessings.** Caught up in what might be regretful, annoying or frustrating about our lives, we often forget what has gone, or is going, right. You can wrap yourself in a warm feeling of comfort if you count what is good. It may seem trivial or small set against your complaints, but it can persuade you that, if those issues are a source of comfort, there will be others.

▶ **Pick your people.** Some people in our lives are toxic. The friend who demands and never gives – who expects you to listen to their tales of woe but is never there when you need comfort, or who criticizes and brings you down on the pretext of being 'honest'. Or the family member who tells you what to do and never listens to your feelings or thoughts. Sometimes we have to maintain some sort of contact... but it can be less than you think it has to be. You deserve people around you who lift you up, not those who bring you down.

▶ **Tell yourself how you value yourself – and spread the love.** Being valued is the most important thing. Being valued should go hand in hand with being loved or liked, but you can be valued without either of those, and it's what makes you feel cherished. Hearing someone say 'I love you' is marvellous, but so, too, is 'You did a really good job of that' or 'I do appreciate what you've done there.' But as well as being valued by other people we need to be valued by ourselves; otherwise their appreciation can fall on deaf ears. Think how deflating it can be when you show you value someone and all they can say is: 'It was nothing.' It's not modest – it's an insult to your assessment of them, and it doesn't help them either. You need to recognize your own worth, and congratulate yourself for the person you are and the things you do. And then you can graciously accept other people's appreciation, and give your own. Giving value is a bit like throwing a pebble in pond – it ripples out, affecting everyone.

▶ **Don't compare yourself with others.** You should never say
to a child 'Why can't you be like so-and-so' or 'You did that
so much better than...' It doesn't build competitiveness;
it builds rivalry and resentment, and often leads to people
giving up. In the same way, you should never compare
yourself to anyone else: 'I'm so useless – I can't do it as well
as so-and-so...' or 'I wish I were like...' You are your own
unique being with your own unique abilities, strengths and
opportunities. Celebrate that.

▶ **Don't believe that everyone has to like you.** You don't
like everyone, and the sky does not fall. In fact, your likes
or dislikes can have no effect whatsoever on them – they
manage without your approval. In the same vein, don't feel
that everyone has to like you or it's a disaster. I'm not with
the Roman emperor Caligula who said, 'Let them hate me
as long as they fear me,' but the reality is that you'd prefer
some people in your life to respect rather than like you, and it
wouldn't hurt you if some were neutral or indifferent. Strive
to please everyone you know and, not only will you become
vulnerable and needy, but you may well alienate the people
who do matter. Prioritize the people who matter to you –
they're the only ones whose feelings about you are relevant.

▶ **Do your best.** We can't all be gold-medal or Nobel Prize
winners, or chief executives or Oscar contenders. What we
can all do, however, is our best. Giving up or becoming bitter
and frustrated because you can't be the best denies you the
chance to shine in your own way. Just as we should never tell
children their efforts are wasted unless they get the top prize,
we need to recognize for ourselves that doing the best we can
is no less a triumph. We do, however, have to do that – do
the very best we can, with full effort and complete focus.
And we should reward and congratulate ourselves when we
achieve a personal best, even when it might not stack up
against what other people can achieve. Your best is your best
and you can't ask for more.

▶ **Be in the now.** The upside of looking back at the regrets
we have can be that we take the lessons we can draw from
them to make ourselves and our lives better. One drawback,

however, is that we can get fixed either in the past or in the future – what it was like and how we want it to be. We can get into the habit as parents of always looking forward, too – 'Won't it be wonderful when he can walk and talk / can manage certain things for herself / becomes a teenager?' Teenagers can spend most of their adolescence longing to be older – to be mature and independent. We can even do it on a trivial basis, longing for summer to come and our holiday, or for winter with its festivities. It can all set a tone for always feeling that any other time but this is desirable. A vital part of cherishing yourself is also cherishing the moment. Enjoy the *now* – this year, this month, this day, this moment. In fact, even if what you're experiencing at present isn't so good, still make the effort to be in the now rather than wishing your life away.

▶ **Be kind.** People who are kind and helpful to others have been shown to be happier and healthier. If you're spreading happiness, you're less likely to be dwelling on past regrets and more likely to be avoiding future ones. And you'll be looking after yourself as well as other people. Being kind makes you feel good. It also means that your kindness is likely to come winging its way back to you, sometime.

'Do not regret growing older. It is a privilege denied to many.'
Anon.

Remember this: Points to consider

▶ The 'Ten easy steps to fitness' can be a user manual for you. Do as many as you can, or need, to do.

▶ The Action Plan can do for your mind and feelings what the 'Ten steps' can do for your body and health.

▶ Learn to accept yourself and to be positive. Look to the future and don't waste time and emotional energy on dark thoughts of what might have been in the past.

▶ Accept yourself, forget about comparisons with others, and do the best you can to be who you really want to be.

Focus points

✱ Looking back and dwelling on bad health choices, or on having made none, is not going to help you achieve new ambitions. Be positive, live in the now and look forward to the future.

✱ In all your health and fitness matters, first decide what is important and what you can realistically hope to achieve.

✱ There are few short cuts to health and fitness, whatever the magazines promise.

✱ Take those 'Ten steps'.

✱ Step 7 of your Action Plan can be a useful guide to looking after your inner self – your mind and your feelings.

✱ Find what your real talent is. Forget how people have viewed you – or you have viewed yourself – in the past and develop your full potential now.

✱ Appreciate what you already have and also appreciate yourself. Then you will really be able to make things better.

✱ The Action Plan does not insist that you do everything. Do what you can, or what you really need to do.

✱ Accepting yourself for what you really are is the key to starting out on your journey to where you might like to be.

✱ You can only do your best. Don't aim at an unachievable perfection – more satisfaction is to be gained in getting to an achievable 'good enough' state.

Next step

The next and final chapter looks at how you can use your regrets as a spur to make changes in your life, how and when to say sorry, and when to forgive or let go of regret.

9

'So what can I do about it?'

In this chapter you will learn:

▶ *How to decide if your regrets do need attending to*

▶ *About identifying your regrets and prioritizing action*

▶ *How and when to say 'sorry'*

▶ *About resolving regrets by making changes, forgiving or letting go.*

Taking action

> 'Make the most of your regrets; never smother your sorrow, but tend and cherish it till it comes to have a separate and integral interest. To regret deeply is to live afresh.'
>
> Henry David Thoreau

We've explored that we all have regrets, and that they can be an encumbrance, holding us back from being happy or achieving what we want in our lives. But some people find regrets less destructive – they have the resilience to put regrets in their place, to laugh at them and see them as futile. As one of my questionnaire respondents, when asked what she might have changed, said: 'And herein lies the rub – you go back and change something and everything else changes, too, including all the good parts of your life that you don't regret.' Sometimes the best decision is to accept what happened in your past, shrug and soldier on. Others use their regrets as a spur to making beneficial changes in the here and now, and for the future.

I asked people in my questionnaire whether they had particular regrets about their childhood, teens, twenties, thirties, forties and fifties. What was noticeable was that regrets did multiply as people got older. Clearly, for some people regrets recede as they get their lives into some perspective and, perhaps with maturity and hindsight, felt more in control and in charge. But, for many, what hindsight brings is a chance to look back and think 'If only I had... I wouldn't be where I am now, and that would be a good thing!' For others, maturity brings a sense of panic as what might be the midpoint of their lives is reached and passed. With increasingly less before us than behind us, as we begin the downhill slide, there might be a feeling that it is too late to do anything about the issues that sadden, frustrate or annoy us. Wrong turns have been taken and there is no going back.

But, as we've already seen, you can pull together a plan – a map for the future to identify your regrets and how you might address them to avoid sadness in your future.

What can you do? – revisit your Action Plan

In this, our final, chapter then, I want you to revisit your Action Plan. After all, the whole point of this book is not so much to mull over the past but to create a workable strategy for the future.

STEP 1: IDENTIFY YOUR MAIN REGRETS

You might think this through on your own or you might use family and friends to discuss an issue. You'll find that very few people, when faced with the issue, have nothing to say. As already mentioned, regrets can form part of an edifice – the structure of your life that might be mixed with high and low points. If you could wish one part away, it may bring mixed results. Gray said:

> 'I had such a crap childhood – I mean really awful. Violent father, a mother more concerned with getting her own crap together than taking care of her kids. I was bright and my school expected me to go to university but I arsed around too much and left with few qualifications. So I left home, worked in various ways for a year, then one of my old friends said I should come up to the university town he was in, doss at his house and do my A levels again at a local college. Well, I did, and got good results and then a university place, and finally I ended up where I am now – with a good job. And I met the love of my life through people at that college. So, if I hadn't gone this route thanks to my childhood I'd never have met her. We celebrate our 40th wedding anniversary next year. I can't wish away my childhood – I can't change a thing because it led to her.'

But one way Gray's regrets over his childhood did help him was to focus intently on being a good father and husband:

> 'Yeah, we've had our moments – what marriage doesn't? And sometimes I could just murder my kids. But I've never been complacent about being a dad and a husband. Every time I feel like storming out I just think of my dad and mum, and I come right back and fix it. I think about it. I always try to do better.'

Using ideas-storming, you can put your finger on what it was that you wish had been different, and look at what message that might have for you. It might be about any of the following:

▶ **The ability to communicate with your partner** Talking with someone important in your life is a skill you learn – from observing your own parents and from experience as you form friendships as a child and a teenager and then a young adult. Like riding a bike, it's a skill you have to acquire, not a talent you're born with, and one which, if you haven't had the luck to have learned it easily and over a period of years, you might need some crash courses in later on. Being honest, being open, listening as well as talking, are all part of it, and, if you need to brush up on your skills, organizations such as Relate could help. (See Appendix.)

▶ **Parenting skills** If your own parenting left something to be desired, you might long to go back and change it. You can't – but you can become both the parent to yourself you always wanted, and be helped to be the parent you wished you'd had to your own children. Organizations such as Family Lives offer the chance to talk this through, and to participate in Parents Together courses, online or face to face, to learn how.

▶ **The ability to make choices rather than drifting into decisions** Not making a choice – waiting and delaying, avoiding and denying – is as much a decision as making one. Letting it happen means accepting whatever course is imposed by events or other people – but you're still making that choice, to let outside influences impose on you. People often say that their fate is sealed, that it's destiny, luck or karma that dictates what happens to you, or that you had no control over events. Now you are an adult you have far more power than you imagine to steer the course of your life. With that responsibility might come anxiety and guilt. But with it could come fewer regrets.

▶ **The recognition that you need to answer calls, be in touch, look after family connections and friendships** Being disconnected – without the safety net of a network of people who care about you – can leave you feeling vulnerable and alone. What many people with regrets over this issue recognize is that you have to make efforts to make and keep those networks alive – calling and returning calls, making time to see and interact with the people you know. It's like servicing a car. If you leave your car neglected on the roadside for months, it won't start when you want it to. And if you forget to put in oil or fuel or keep the tyres inflated, it will come to a halt. Relationships are the same – they need to be run around the block every now and then and fuelled with a coffee or a meal.

▶ **Prioritizing your time and attention** Those who shout the loudest tend to be looked after. So, children and insistent friends or family may claim the lion's share of your time while a patient partner or a better friend or loving family member stand in line and maybe never get your attention. We know how to prioritize our time at work – decide which are the important jobs and do them first. You need to do the same in your private life – decide who needs your time, decide who you would like to give your time to, decide how much time you have, then apportion your time and keep to your plan. If someone low or not on your list calls, say: 'I can't talk now; no, sorry, can't do that – goodbye!'

▶ **Looking after yourself and your needs** When you're allocating your time and attention, put in a share for yourself. Think of the coffee cup. If you're sitting sipping your coffee and your partner or a child or friend comes rushing up to you and says 'Can I have some?' what would you answer? If your cup is full to the brim, you can say, 'Yes, of course! Help yourself!', and feel fine about it – there's plenty left for you. If it's half full you might say 'Well, OK. But please leave some for me – it's almost gone.' And if your cup is down to the dregs, you have to say, regretfully or with annoyance: 'No, sorry. There's none left for either of us.'

Imagine yourself as that coffee cup. You might be full to the brim with energy and love, and with time on your hands to give attention as required. Or you might feel distracted, tired, able to help but on the edge. Or you might feel drained – depleted of anything for yourself and so unable to cope with looking after anyone else. You need to look after yourself because you deserve as much as anyone else to be satisfied, cared for, valued. If doing it for yourself isn't enough, then recognize that, if you don't take care of your own needs, you won't be fit and able to take care of anyone else.

▶ **Being in the moment** Focus on being in the present, and enjoying this, here, now. If you spend your whole time looking forward or back, you are never going to achieve contentment.

▶ **The strength to seek help when you need it** You're not alone, so don't make the mistake of thinking you have to struggle on if your life feels difficult. Look through the Appendix for all of the excellent organizations out there ready and able to help you. And, if these organizations are running, recognize that it must be because you're not the only one feeling like this.

STEP 2: SAY SORRY

Apologies are often necessary because the regret you have is holding you back. It could mean apologizing to someone else – someone close to you who you see often or can get in contact with. Or it might be to someone far away or even out of reach. And, of course, the person you may need to say sorry to could be you, for opportunities neglected and chances let go. Strangely, it's not only the big issues we might play over and over in our minds and feel that we'd like to go back and redress. Small niggles can sometimes loom large. We need to pay attention because they can mask a bigger worry, and it's that we may need to focus on – the small issue serves as the warning sign. Saying sorry may mean doing any of the following:

▶ **Doing it face to face** If you've an apology to make, it's hardest of all to do it face to face – it might feel a lot safer to do it by phone or text or using some other long-distance method. But face to face has many advantages, not least that it allows the other person to make it a dialogue, perhaps to apologize to you, too, and certainly to draw the encounter to a conclusion. It's much more likely to end with you feeling better, whereas holding the situation at arm's length may still leave you feeling unsatisfied.

▶ **Taking responsibility for what we say** Whether you write or speak your apology, the key is to say 'I' and take responsibility for what you say – not '*You* might need an apology' but 'I want to say I'm sorry.'

▶ **Listening to the other person** You should never make assumptions about what the other person thinks or feels, or how they saw what happened. They may have some apologizing to do, too, or they may need to check out with you how you saw it. Good communication is always two-way – you listen as much as you talk.

▶ **Offering amends** Making amends can be as simple as the apology itself, or restitution you can talk over with the other person or that suggests itself to you.

▶ **Making changes** Regrets may be about the past but what those memories from our childhood or early adulthood most often do, and with the most damage, is leave us with issues in our present and future. You may be sad and sorry about the fact that one or both of your parents were never there for you, but the significant effect is that it gave you no good model on which to base your own parenting, which means that, much as you don't want to, you could follow their pattern and do the same. Equally, a bad example may make it hard for you to manage good, intimate and loving relationships – the pattern you follow is of holding the ones you would like to love at arm's length. So, more than saying sorry, the best thing you can do to overcome regret is consider how it affected you and how it might in the future, and address those issues. Look at the way you manage your relationships with your friends and family and learn lessons. Do it differently from the way it was done to you, and look for advice and help on doing so.

▶ **Forgiving or letting go** If what happened makes it hard for you to forgive, the best advice is at least to let it go. Anger, bitterness and recriminations hurt you as badly as, if not more than, the person you hold the grudge against – don't do their work for them all over again.

Case study: Tom

'I had serious regrets around the fact that my dad was hardly ever there – he worked away from home when I was young and when he was based with us he worked long hours. When I had my own children I was determined not to do the same. But two things have, well, if not made me forgive him at least helped me understand him better and let it go. One is that he's trying so hard now to be a good granddad, and by doing that has actually been quite a good dad. The other is that I can see how hard you have to fight even in this day and age to fit work and life together.'

STEP 3: CONFRONT AND ACCEPT WHAT HAS LED TO YOUR REGRETS

Being able to identify, not just exactly what are your regrets, but from where they originated, can help you banish them. Once you know, for instance, that your lack of confidence comes from somebody in your past telling you that you were stupid or useless, you can confront those fears you've internalized and return them to the sender. You can isolate the voice that whispers criticism and denigration and banish it. You can either subject it to the cold light of day by talking it through with the people who love you now, or hold a ceremony to ritually cleanse yourself of their influence.

Case study: Carole

'I always used to get so furious with my husband for his lack of confidence. He's a super bloke – kind and capable and downright lovely. But ask him to stand up in front of people and talk and he went to pieces. I never could understand it, until I met his grandmother, who was a grade-A bitch and a bully. Seb had avoided her at the time I first knew him until we got married, when we had to invite her. She shocked me – at our wedding she was cold and critical of me, gave Seb a dressing-down for what he was wearing, and laid into one of our friend's children for running around and enjoying himself. I bit my lip but I had a word later with Seb's mother – this was his dad's mum.

And the next time we saw his grandmother, at someone else's wedding, I took her aside, told her I thought she was a poisonous little bitch, that she had wrecked Seb's confidence and that she wasn't going to do it any more. Nor was she going to have a single chance at doing it to our kids – she was barred. Well, I thought she would have a fit but I didn't care! His dad rang me later to say that it was the best thing I'd ever done and that he was following suit, at last. And Seb just blossomed overnight once he knew I had backed him and both his parents backed him and that it wasn't his fault after all.'

Confronting regrets doesn't always mean confronting people, but it can mean taking action to stop whatever it was that led to your unhappiness continuing to affect you.

STEP 4: CONSIDER YOUR RELATIONSHIPS

Your regrets may begin with your parents and continue through family, friends, partners and children. So often, an insecure foundation may leave you feeling vulnerable in close relationships so that you have unrealistically low or high expectations of yourself and those who relate to you. Frequently, having not been trusted or respected, we cannot trust or respect ourselves. As an agony aunt, I get so many letters from people who discard friends or partners, not because they want to, but because someone has told them that person should go. Other letters come from people who stay in clearly toxic relationships, whether social or intimate, because they don't have the strength of their own convictions that this isn't doing them any good.

Key idea: You don't have to give all the time

Just because someone demands something of you doesn't mean you have to give it – whether it's time, attention or a relationship.

Your relationships don't need to be bland or non-confrontational to be healthy. Even the best friends or partners, parents or children in healthy relationships disagree at times, and arguments can be heated and difficult. But the sign of a good relationship is where you can communicate and find some resolution to your differences, not that you don't have them. If you keep experiencing the same pattern of dysfunctional

relationship, always finding yourself with people who abuse
you or who are overly needy or possessive, or where you find
yourself getting to a certain stage in a relationship and suddenly
losing interest, it's likely that you are replaying the scenario
you've inherited at some point in your childhood, and need to
give it some scrutiny. A professional counsellor could help you
identify what and why you are replaying, and aid you in making
changes to avoid these repetitive patterns. (See Appendix.)

STEP 5: GRIEVE FOR YOUR REGRETS
Weep, wail, rend your clothing – often we can't move on from
our regrets until we have not only identified them, apologized
and faced up to who might be responsible for them, but also
mourned them. We don't often do grief very well in the West –
it's all too embarrassing and inelegant. But the reality is that
to move on and make sense of how we feel about those bits of
our past that come back to haunt us, we might need to make
a fuss. Regrets need to be… well, regretted. We need to accept
that it's OK to feel strongly about these issues, to be angry and
bitter and miserable about them. It's only when we can accept
this that can we begin to heal and leave behind those negative
emotions that hold us back.

We often keep feeling regrets, and keep replaying all the issues
around them, because we're stuck in one or several of the stages
of mourning. Mourning is a process, and in order to reach the
last stage, that of acceptance, and to heal from our grief, we
have to embrace and experience and then let go of all the seven
stages in the process. We need to go through these steps:

1 **Shock and denial** – when we can't believe that whatever led
   to our regret happened, and try to pretend it didn't

2 **Pain** – sharp, often searing pain at memories you may not
   want to remember

3 **Guilt** – that it might have been your fault, that there was
   something you could have done or not done to stop it
   happening

4 **Anger** – at yourself or at whoever caused your regrets

5 **Bargaining** – when you promise yourself you'll do or not do something in the hope that this will reverse the situation

6 **Depression and loneliness** – when your regret seems to be something you'll have to endure

7 **Hope** – when you begin to feel that maybe you won't feel so awful for ever

8 and, finally, **acceptance**.

But stay with anger or guilt, or indeed any of the stages, or cycle back and forth between several of them and you stay stuck in the grieving process. That's why, however much you might think it natural to go on feeling angry at someone, or find it hard to let go of guilt, letting go and moving on are the only things that are good for you. You don't necessarily do it to forgive someone who has harmed you. You do it to stop allowing them go on doing so.

STEP 6: LEARN FROM YOUR REGRETS

Considering regrets would be a futile and possibly dangerous project if all you were going to do is call them to mind. The real purpose is to explore your regrets and learn how to make them work for you. If you can identify what they are about and what you can do in another way to minimize them, you will have done yourself and possibly other people a service.

Regret serves a function – to sound the warning bell about issues you wished had been different. It allows you to have some insight into yourself and what makes you tick, and motivate you to make changes. They are a spur to action, and a signpost to what that action ought to be. Never regret your regrets – they are, as has been said, experience. The trick is to turn those experiences to your advantage, even if they seemed at the time to be distinctly negative. You might ask yourself:

▶ What is my regret?

▶ What has been the effect of the experience or situation I regret?

▶ What changes should I make to turn this around?

Case study: Mel

Mel asked for my help because, although she had a responsible job with a good salary, she felt dissatisfied. She had done well at school and university and was climbing up the corporate ladder. What emerged when she did consider her regrets was that she had longed as a teenager to do voluntary service and to travel. She'd had plenty of foreign holidays, but none had satisfied her desire to go off the beaten track. She was horrified at the suggestion that perhaps she needed to go back and do this now. It would derail her career, and she was too old to go roughing it around the world – it was out of the question. And then she started making enquiries and found several charities begging for people with her experience and seniority. Mel discovered that her own company would give her a year's sabbatical and would even sponsor her. She spent nine months working on a project in China, three months travelling with a group of people she met there, and returned to find that not only had it not harmed her career, but it had enhanced it. She also now serves as a trustee of the charity she worked with, and is working on her list of other regrets – never having got fit enough to run a marathon, never having learned to speak French, being only a middling cook.

Key idea: It's not as hard as you think!

Sometimes the deepest and most ambitious longings left over from your youth can be fulfilled – and then you find that some of the others aren't so hard after all. All it takes is to consider them.

Remember this: Points to consider

▶ Most of us need to do something about our regrets, either to turn and face them and make changes or to put them in perspective.

▶ Letting decisions happen to you is as much a choice as grasping the nettle and being decisive.

▶ The seven-step Action Plan given in this book is just that – a move-by-move plan that you can take at your own pace and in your own time.

▶ Prioritize, then do things when and how they best suit you.

Try it now: Fill a jar with 'good things'

Every time something good happens, write a brief note about it and slip the paper in a jar. Include everything, from big events such as birthday parties or special celebrations, to praise from your partner, a friend or at work, to simply seeing a lovely sunset or hearing a bird sing. Watch the jar get full. On New Year's Eve, or whenever you feel down, empty the jar and read out the slips. We often forget all the little things that cheer us up and make life enjoyable, and sometimes we even forget the big things if feeling bad gets in the way. This simple idea can help you remind yourself that life is also full of good moments.

STEP 7: CHERISH YOURSELF

Most of us like it when someone else does something nice for us, and makes us feel loved, valued and special. And most of us know how to do the same to the people we love. But the majority of us are truly terrible at turning the same thought and concern on ourselves. We put ourselves second in line for everything, we accept stress and pressure and we run ourselves ragged. The problem is that, if we're wrung out and wasted, we can't actually look after everyone else to the best of our ability. And, far more importantly, we're not giving ourselves a fair chance.

We deserve to be looked after, too, and the first step in allowing other people to care for us is to look after ourselves, and thus recognize that we deserve it. First, let's look at the ways to show care for others:

▷ **Say we love and value them.** We often think the people we love know how we feel about them, and that's enough. It's good, but it's certainly not enough. Tell them that you like them, love them and value them as often as possible. It never gets tired, it never gets boring, no matter how much a partner wriggles and says we don't have to do so or a child says 'Oh, Muuum / Daaad, don't be so embarrassing!' I've never had a correspondent or a face-to-face client complain: 'Oh, it was awful, my mum/dad was always there for me and never stopped telling me they loved me!' I've had more than I can count say the opposite, though.

- **Thank them.** We say please and thank you to colleagues or even strangers, but so often we forget to say it out loud to those nearest us – we assume they know it or don't have to hear it. They do – say it!

- **Do something for them.** Something as simple as making a coffee, their favourite meal, or doing a chore they hate tells the people we love that we do cherish them. It's called 'a stroke', and we need to give them strokes as frequently as possible. Think of the strokes you can give, and show them how to give strokes to you, too.

Try it now: Practise RAKs

Practise Random Acts of Kindness. It doesn't take much to spread a little happiness. Hold a door open for the next person, let the person behind you in the queue go ahead if they're in a hurry or their basket is less full than yours, donate blood, say hello to people… Random Acts of Kindness are catching. You do one and that person may well be inspired to do something similar. It spread like the ripples in a pond…

Give them something. Gifts are the traditional way of saying we value someone – gifts at birthdays or feast days or at the beginning of a weekend. But you don't have to spend money to give someone something they'd love and that they know shows they are held in your heart – a note, text, email or video greeting to say so, a bunch of flowers picked from your own garden or the garden of someone who has given you permission to do so, or a well-chosen picture or video sent in an email or text or posted on a social network site.

Spend time with them. There's no substitute for time spent together – doing things, chatting or just hanging out. And when you're not actually together, keep up the link through media – texting, posting, messaging.

See the upside, in them and for them. You can show the people close to you that you love and value them by respecting and trusting them – by always seeing their good side no matter how annoyed you may feel with them. Always see 'bad' behaviour as a way of saying they feel bad rather than being about their badness. And always label the behaviour, not them – so say 'I'm annoyed you didn't tidy up – do it now and then tell me about your day' rather than 'You lazy git! I told you to do that...' And that then means helping them to be optimistic and to look for solutions rather than problems.

Case study: Denny and Sal

Denny's friend Sal was always complaining and bitching about his job until several of their mutual friends had taken to avoiding him. So the next time he started, Denny said: 'Sal, you're clearly not happy, so why don't we see what we can do to change things?' By being relentlessly upbeat and refusing to let Sal fall back into complaints, Denny got him to consider his own abilities, what the job offered and what it did not and so on until Sal decided that what he needed to do was to offer his boss a plan to improve the situation. If that didn't work, he was going to leave. To his surprise, his boss was delighted with his suggestions and took them all on board – and promoted Sal to implement them.

'Burn the candles, use the nice sheets, wear the fancy lingerie. Don't save it for a special occasion. Today is special.'

Regina Brett

Seeing the ways we can show other people that we care, how can we show equal care for ourselves? Here are some ways:

▶ **Value ourselves.** We don't always value ourselves. We focus on our own bad points – our clumsiness, our inability to speak in public, our fat butts. A useful exercise is to tell a friend or family member all the things you like about them, and ask them to do the same for you – you'll find they can see your good points, and so should you. So spend a moment thinking about these and all the things you do well, and praise yourself for them.

▶ **Thank ourselves.** You do good things for other people and maybe they thank you – but you should spare a thank you for yourself every now and then. When you see how good it makes you feel, that should give you every motivation to do it to other people, and that gives them the incentive to do it back to you. The motto here is 'Pass it on' – because it all comes back to you in the end.

▶ **Do something nice for ourselves.** You deserve that cup of something hot, that chance to sit down and read a magazine, that ten minutes with your earphones in listening to your choice of music. You deserve to be the one making the choice of what you do tonight, this weekend, next holiday. Be kind to yourself because you deserve it.

▶ **Give ourselves something.** This is of course the source of all those shopping trips – the often thwarted or guilty desire to make yourself feel cherished and valued by buying yourself a new outfit, a new object. If this is the only way you spoil yourself, it can get out of hand and can actually be cripplingly expensive but also unsatisfying. What is vital is to understand you're doing it to make yourself feel good – important, the centre of someone's attention, cared for. If you pay attention to the other ways of cherishing yourself, then you can indulge the occasional shopping spree within boundaries and without breaking the bank. And you can look for cheaper ways of doing it, too. If the impulse is to give yourself a stroke through a treat, an inexpensive bunch of flowers or new brand of coffee, something from a charity shop or bought cheaply online will do the trick just as well as something from a designer shop.

▶ **Spend time with ourselves.** Having time with family and friends is important, and we shouldn't minimize it. But it's also central to looking after yourself to sometimes have time with yourself, for yourself, doing some of the things you like to do, alone. Your fitness and exercise may be something you can lay claim to as private time – running or walking, going to a gym, cycling. You might want to stake out a claim to being left alone for a period so that you can listen to music, have a hot bath, read, watch a programme only you like, or simply sitting with a drink and thinking. You are good company – enjoy it.

▶ **See the upside, in yourself and for yourself.** Just as you'd give other people the benefit of your trust and respect, you need to do the same for yourself. Probably the most pernicious aspect of having regrets is that they often leave us distrusting our own abilities or reactions and lacking respect for our own skills. Considering and acting on our regrets is the chance you have to overturn these tendencies – to go forward with optimism and a renewed confidence in yourself. Take a moment every day to think over what you do well, what skills you have, what abilities and talents. And give yourself the opportunity to use them.

If you could go back, what advice would you have for your younger self?

I asked my questionnaire respondents what they might like to tell their younger selves. Here are some of the answers:

> 'Like yourself more. All young people – with very few exceptions – are beautiful. Male and female. Don't worry so much about how you look – you're gorgeous and will never be this good again so enjoy!'

> 'Have a go at everything that's offered – apart from the bad stuff! Seize opportunities, get out there and make your own. Don't put life off to "do another day". This might just be your last.'

> 'Listen to others who have more experience. Read. Think about your future and plan ahead. Money is important so don't disregard the need to collect a bit along the way. Don't let other people make major decisions for you. Always keep one hand on the wheel.'

> 'Gather as many friends as you can and treasure them.'

> 'Believe in yourself!'

> 'Be kind to yourself. Give your dreams a chance. Listen to advice and accept help. Don't just blindly go with the flow, balance the opportunities which come up against your own goals: will they draw you closer to who you want to become? Don't waste your talents.'

> 'Don't lie. To yourself or others. The consequences of lying are always worse. And tell people when something is wrong.'

> 'Talk about it, no matter how stupid you think something sounds or will make you sound. Talking about it will help. It is not stupid if it is affecting you.'

'I would tell my 13-year-old self to read lots of books on feminism. And not to quit German!'

'Don't run with your arms crossed.'

'Do more. Work harder, talk to people more rather than relying on texting etc., write to people more and forgive the little things.'

'Think. Think. Think. Always ask yourself: is this really true? Do I believe this? Is this what you want to base your life on, let alone your behaviour this week or this month? How do you want to look back on this decision? By all means, listen to everyone, gather new ideas, but use your intelligence. There is no reason to think anyone knows better than you – but be selective and pick out the wheat from the chaff; don't be dismissive. Think! Believe in your own fundamental compassion and desire to do the right thing – but think hard about what that right thing is. Think, think, think!'

'I would tell myself: there's a big happy world out there; it's not all filled with mean people or exploitative people. I would tell myself that I, and my needs, and my time, were just as valuable as anyone else's. I would tell myself I could say no, and the world wouldn't end and I wouldn't be less loved by those who loved me.'

'I would tell myself that I am a worthwhile person, and that it doesn't matter what others think of me.'

'That you do deserve to be happy but that you can't rely on others to make you happy – that happiness and being satisfied with your lot is up to you and that only you can change things. It might seem reasonable to want others to adapt or compromise, but sometimes what they want is just going to steamroll right over you and your dreams – you either pick yourself up and walk away, or you lie there and let them do it over and over again. It is up to you.'

And perhaps my favourite:

'For goodness' sake, ASK HIM OUT!'

Try it now: What advice would you have for
your younger self?

▶ This is a useful exercise to do for yourself. Ideas-storm, either on your
own or, preferably, with others.

▶ Remember the rules – throw everything that comes to mind on to
paper with no holding back, discussing or arguing, and use other
people's ideas to inspire more of your own.

▶ Once you have a full list, talk it over. What pointers could this give
you for you to make some decisions, and know the areas you'd like to
work on?

Focus points

✳ Your first decision is to decide if your regrets do need attention or if you can deal with the past happily and are prepared to just soldier on.

✳ If action is needed, start by identifying your regrets and then prioritize how and what you are going to do about them.

✳ You can use the Action Plan as a guide to identifying your regrets and deciding where you are with them at the moment.

✳ Not having apologized properly can be a major reason for why a regret is still holding you back. The Action Plan will show you how and when to say 'sorry'.

✳ Making changes, forgiving and letting go are other major requirements if regrets are to be resolved.

✳ All of us are in relationships of some kind – with our family, partner, friends or other people. These will need to be looked at and made healthy if resolving regrets is to be successful.

✳ The real purpose of considering our regrets is to explore them and learn from them. It can be futile, and even dangerous, if all you do is call them to mind and suffer anguish over them.

✳ We all deserve to be looked after and cherished. The first step in allowing others to care for us is to look after ourselves and give ourselves a fair chance in life.

✳ Start really believing in yourself. This will help develop the self-confidence you need to go forward effectively.

✳ The worst thing about regrets is that they can leave you distrusting your own abilities and worth. Dealing with them is your chance to kill these doubts and to go forward with confidence.

Final word

As I said in my introduction, regrets can hobble you not only because of the resentment and pain that thinking about what went wrong may cause you but also by setting you on the road to making the same mistakes that led to the regrets in the first place. The playwright Arthur Miller said: 'Maybe all one can do is hope to end up with the right regrets.' And maybe he was right. You can set your mind on forging on and overriding your regrets and, if you have the resilience to do so, that may be what works for you.

The author D.H. Lawrence, however, said: 'I want to live my life so that my nights are not full of regrets,' and to do so, sometimes we have to go back first, deal with our regrets, both to put them in perspective and in their place, and shrug off the malign influence they may have over us. Living so you have little to regret is definitely the best option and that is what I hope I might have helped you do. Considering your regrets should be the opportunity to make better choices – to look back with forgiveness and understanding and to look forward with inspiration and determination.

One of my respondents told me:

> 'My husband and I visited Cornwall 35 years ago and swore we'd retire there because it was so beautiful. Soon after a much loved uncle died. He was two years off retirement and had spent the previous five years telling my aunt they'd do this, go there, enjoy that when he retired. She did all the things they'd been promising themselves, but on her own. I looked at my husband and decided I didn't want that to happen to us. We gave up lucrative jobs to move down six months later. We've worked hard with a business of our own and at times it's been a struggle – we certainly haven't had as successful a life, financially speaking, as we would have had if we'd waited until later to make the move. But we've had 25 years of living where we really wanted, doing what we really want, and I wouldn't change a moment of it. Regrets? No, we have no regrets. Aren't we lucky?!'

I wish you that luck, too!

Appendix: A list of organizations that can provide help

Your own GP may offer a counselling service or, if not, will be able to refer you to a counsellor.

Family Lives
This national charity offers help and support in all aspects of family lives and relationships. The website has information and advice and access to an email service, a helpline and live chat with help and advice for parents and young people. The charity also offers face-to-face support groups and workshops and extended support for complex or difficult issues.

Helpline is free, 24/7, even on mobiles: 0808 800 2222
familylives.org.uk
You can also Skype via the website.
Personalized email service at parentsupport@familylives.org.uk

Relate
Through local centres, Relate offers relationship counselling and life-skills courses for couples, individuals and young people. Counselling is also available over the telephone or through the website.

www.relate.org.uk
Telephone 0300 100 1234

British Association for Counselling and Psychotherapy
The association can suggest a counsellor in your area online at their website or via post.

British Association for Counselling and Psychotherapy
BACP House, 15 St John's Business Park, Lutterworth,
Leicestershire LE17 4HB
www.bacp.co.uk

The Institute of Family Therapy

The institute helps with family problems. Write to:

24–32 Stephenson Way, London NW1 2HX.
www.instituteoffamilytherapy.org.uk
Tel: 0207 391 9150

Mind

Mind is the leading mental health charity in England and Wales, providing a mental health information service to people by phone, email or letter. It offers support and understanding and information on where to get help, drug treatments, alternative therapies and advocacy.

www.mind.org.uk
0300 123 3393

Young Minds

This charity is committed to improving children's mental health, by educating parents and carers in the importance of recognizing when a child is troubled and providing adequate support for these children before their problems escalate out of control. They provide a helpline and information for parents and young people.

www.youngminds.org.uk
Helpline: 0808 802 5544

Sane

This charity provides emotional support, practical help and information while also raising mental health awareness.

www.sane.org.uk
Helpline 0845 767 8000

Citizens' Advice Bureau

This is an independent organization providing free, confidential and impartial advice on all subjects to anyone. The address and telephone number of your local CAB can be found in the telephone directory or on their website. There is also advice online on their website.

www.citizensadvice.org.uk

Money Advice Service
This service offers free independent advice on financial issues.

www.moneyadviceservice.org.uk
03000 500 5000

Family Mediators Association
The FMA can put you in touch with trained mediators who work with both parents and children.

www.thefma.co.uk
National helpline: 0800 200 0033

National Family Mediation
An umbrella organization for local family mediation services, NFM can also provide details of local services in the UK.

www.nfm.org.uk
0300 4000 636

Care for the Family
This national charity aims to promote strong family life and to help those who face family difficulties.

www.careforthefamily.org.uk/

Cruse Bereavement Care
Promotes the wellbeing of bereaved people and enables anyone affected by death to understand their grief and cope with their loss. The organization provides counselling and support, information, advice, education and training services.

www.crusebereavementcare.org.uk
Helpline: 0844 477 9400

The Samaritans
The Samaritans are available 24 hours a day to listen to people in distress and to provide emotional support.

www.samaritans.org
Email: jo@samaritans.org
Helpline: 08457 90 90 90

Infertility Network
This charity offers advice, support and understanding around infertility.

www.infertilitynetworkuk.com

British Pregnancy Advisory Service
The BPAS offers decision-making support and helps with all aspects of counselling both before and after abortion as well as carrying out abortions.

www.bpas.org
08457 30 40 30

Marie Stopes
This is a leading provider of sexual and reproductive healthcare services that includes unplanned pregnancy counselling, abortion, vasectomy and contraception.

www.mariestopes.org.uk
0845 300 8090

UK Parents' Lounge
An online forum for parents.

www.ukparentslounge.com

Parents.com
An online community for parents.

www.parents.com

Mumsnet
This website offers a supportive online community for parents where you can meet other mums in your area and further afield, and find out about local activities.

www.mumsnet.com

Netmums
This parenting website offers local information, expert advice and friendly support, and lets you meet other mums in your area and further afield, and find out about local activities.

www.netmums.com

Grandparents' Association

The Grandparents' Association supports grandparents whose grandchildren are out of contact with them or who have childcare responsibilities for their grandchildren.

www.grandparents-association.org.uk
Helpline: 0845 4349585

Grandparents Plus

Grandparents Plus provides information about research, resources and support for grandparents and those working with grandparents.

www.grandparentsplus.org.uk
Tel: 0300 123 7015

AgeUK

This national charity offers help and advice on all aspects of support for older people, their family members and anyone caring for an older person.

As well as advice and support, they offer Gransnet: http://www.gransnet.com/forums-age-uk – online forums where people can get in contact and chat.

www.ageuk.org.uk
0800 169 6565

Youth Access

The online directory on this website offers advice, information, support and counselling services for young people across the UK.

www.youthaccess.org.uk

National Youth Advocacy Service

NYAS provides advocacy services for children and young people up to the age of 25. They provide specialist help in children's rights, children in care, contact issues, education and youth justice. They have a network of advocates throughout the country and their own legal advice helpline.

www.nyas.net
Email advice for children and young people: help@nyas.net
Free helpline for children and young people: 0300 330 3131

Urban Dictionary
This is an online dictionary constantly updated and defined by users. It's probably the only way of keeping some check on what on earth your teenagers are talking about!

www.urbandictionary.com

The Site
This website for young people has information about a wide range of local services, as well as discussion forums and advice on issues such as moving out.

www.thesite.org

The Hideout
The Hideout is a site for young people worried about domestic violence.

www.thehideout.org.uk

Connexions
Connexions provides information for young people aged 13–19, covering topics such as education and work, health, relationships and housing. They can also provide services by text and email.

www.connexionslive.com

Bullying UK
Part of Family Lives, the national charity that offers help and support in all aspects of family lives, this website has information and advice and access to an email service, helpline, live chat with help and advice for parents and young people. The helpline is free even on mobiles and you can also Skype via the website.

www.bullying.co.uk
Helpline: 0808 800 2222
Email: help@bullying.co.uk

TeenBoundaries
Part of Family Lives, the national charity that offers help and support in all aspects of family lives, TeenBoundaries aims to prevent sexual bullying, peer-on-peer sexual exploitation and promotes positive gender relationships by challenging attitudes and

promoting tolerance, understanding and cohesion between young people. It also offers courses in schools for 11- to 18-year-olds.

teenboundaries.co.uk

Kidscape

Kidscape is a national charity which aims to prevent bullying and abuse of young people aged 16 years or under, and which provides support for their parents/carers.

www.kidscape.org.uk
Helpline: 08451 205 204

Place2Be

Place2Be works in schools providing early-intervention mental health support (including counselling and other services) to young people and their families when and where they need it most.

www.place2be.org.uk

beat (formerly the Eating Disorders Association)

This site provides information, advice and support around eating disorders such as anorexia, bulimia and binge eating.

www.b-eat.co.uk
Email: help@b-eat.co.uk
Helpline: 0845 634 1414
Youthline: 0845 634 7650

PAPYRUS (Parents' Association for the Prevention of Young Suicide)

Papyrus provides information and advice for parents, teachers and healthcare professionals. It aims to raise awareness of young suicide, and many members are parents who have lost a child to suicide. They produce a range of publications and materials.

www.papyrus.org.uk
Helpline: 0800 068 41 41

Brook

This charity provides free and confidential help on contraception and abortion to the under-25s.

Free helpline: 0808 802 1234
www.brook.org.uk

Talk to Frank

Frank provides free and confidential information and advice about drugs. It also has a 24-hour helpline.

www.talktofrank.com
Email: frank@talktofrank.com
Helpline: 0800 77 66 00
SMS 82111

Release

This centre of expertise on drugs and drugs law helps parents when their teenage child has been arrested or cautioned by the police for possession of a drug. They also provide support and legal advice about drug-related issues.

www.release.org.uk
Email: ask@release.org.uk
Helpline: 0845 4500 215

Al-Anon

Al-Anon helps anyone who has a friend or family member with a drinking problem – **Alateen** are there especially for the children of problem drinkers. They can be found at 61 Great Dover Street, London SE1 4YF and on 0207 403 0888.

www.al-anonuk.org.uk

ADFAM

ADFAM works with family members facing problems with drugs or alcohol, to help them gain access to a range of specialized services.

www.adfam.org.uk

Families Need Fathers

This registered charity provides information and support on shared parenting issues arising from family breakdown to divorced and separated parents. Support is provided through a national helpline, a website, a network of volunteers and regular group meetings, held in a variety of locations.

24/7 helpline 0300 0300 363
www.fnf.org.uk

DadTalk and dad.info

An online community for fathers with help, advice, forums and features.

www.dad.info

The Fatherhood Institute
The think-tank on fatherhood offers publications to support fathers and their families.

www.fatherhoodinstitute.org

Homedads
'The only UK support group for stay-at-home dads' has online forums discussing all the issues of being a dad at home with your kids.

www.homedad.org.uk

Separated Dads
This website contains articles and advice for dads living away from their children and offers a regular email newsletter.

www.separateddads.co.uk/

Families and Friends of Lesbians and Gays (FFLAG)
FFLAG provides information and support for parents of lesbian, gay and bisexual young people and their families. They also have local parent support groups, a newsletter, publications and a helpline.

www.fflag.org.uk
Email: info@fflag.org.uk
Helpline: 0845 652 0311

Lesbian and Gay Switchboard
LGS provides advice and support for lesbian and gay people, and their parents.

www.llgs.org.uk
Helpline: 0300 330 0630

Gingerbread
This campaigning organization providess a helpline with free information to lone parents on issues including benefits, tax, legal rights, family law and contact issues, child maintenance and returning to work. They are able to connect lone parents with other organizations and local groups.

Free helpline, on mobiles too: 0808 802 0925
www.gingerbread.org.uk

National Association of Child Contact Centres

The NACCC promotes safe child contact within a national network of child contact centres. A child contact centre is a safe place where children of separated families can spend time with one or both parents and sometimes other family members. Details of local centres can be found on their website or by ringing them.

Telephone: 0845 4500 280
www.naccc.org.uk

Action for Children

This charity supports and helps the UKs most vulnerable and neglected children.

www.actionforchildren.org.uk

CAFCASS (Children and Family Court Advisory and Support Service)

This support service looks after the interests of children and young people involved in cases in the family courts, ensuring that their voices are heard. It helps families to reach agreement over arrangements for their children. CAFCASS only works with families on referral from the court, but their website contains useful information, case studies, advice and contact links.

0844 353 3350
www.cafcass.gov.uk

Parenting Plans – Putting Your Children First: a guide for separating parents

This helpful booklet can be used as an outline for your discussions and agreement. *Parenting Plans* helps you to think of all the things you will need to manage as parents living apart. It contains questions that you could use to trigger discussion on issues such as day-to-day arrangements, holidays, health and money, and includes a section to guide you through what to do if you're finding it hard to agree. You can download this from:
http://tinyurl.com/yavt5s4

Resolution – First for Family Law (the Solicitors Family Law Association)

Resolution gives advice on any family dispute and on issues to do with separation, divorce and new families, and encourages mediation and agreement rather than confrontation.

www.resolution.org.uk

Coram Children's Legal Centre

The centre offers information on all aspects of child law in England and Wales, particularly contact, parental responsibility and residence orders.

Helpline: 08088 020 008 (Mon–Fri 8 a.m.–8 p.m.)
Or speak to an adviser via live webchat.

www.childrenslegalcentre.com

NSPCC

The NSPCC can help with advice on keeping your or any other child safe.

www.nspcc.org.uk
Helpline: 0808 800 5000

ChildLine (now part of the NSPCC)

This is a free confidential helpline for children at risk, open 24 hours.

Freephone: 0800 1111
www.childline.org.uk *or* www.nspcc.org.uk

The Child Exploitation and Online Protection Centre (CEOP)

The centre works across the UK and abroad to tackle child sex abuse wherever and whenever it happens. Part of their strategy for achieving this is by providing Internet safety advice for parents and carers and offering a 'virtual police station' for reporting abuse on the Internet.

ceop.police.uk

Family Rights Group

This is a specialist advice and information service for families in England and Wales, who are in contact with social services concerning the care of their children, and their advisers and supporters.

www.frg.org.uk
Helpline: 0808 801 0366

Terence Higgins Trust

The THT offers a helpline and services for anyone concerned or affected by HIV/AIDS and other STIs. The trust also provides information on welfare rights, legal services, employment and housing as well as counselling and support.

www.tht.org.uk
Helpline: 0808 802 1221

Macmillan Cancer Support
Macmillan improves the lives of people affected by cancer. On their website you can find up-to-date information about cancer as well as practical advice and support for cancer patients, their families and carers.

www.macmillan.org.uk

NHS Choices – End of Life Care
This section of the NHS website offers advice on making decisions and discussing these with family and carers.

www.nhs.uk/Planners/end-of-life-care/Pages/End-of-life-care.aspx

Index

acceptance, 176–7
  of change, 144
  of responsibility, 175
action plans
  acceptance, 82–5, 176–7
  apologizing, 63–71, 174–5
  cherishing yourself, 162–6, 181–5
  grieving, 123–6, 178–9
  identifying regrets, 37–40, 171–4
  learning from regrets, 145–7,
    179–81
  relationships, 99–106, 177–8
active listening, 91
'adult' role, 58
advice
  from others, 132
  to younger self, 185–6
age, effect on regrets, 170
alcohol, 150, 154–5
ambitions
  achieving later in life, 76–80, 85–6
  discouragement, 82–5
  not achieving, 74–5
Angelou, Maya, 44
anger, expressing, 90
anxieties
  analysing, 10
  fear of failure, 12, 75
apologizing, 63–71, 174–5
appreciation, 163–4
  of others, 182–3
approval, need for, 133, 137
arguments
  between friends, 57–8
  resolving, 144
atonement, 175

balancing time, 16–19, 28, 24–32, 54
barriers to achieving goals, 78–80

blame, directed towards self, 14–15,
  40–41, 104
body image, 162
Botox, 159
Brett, Regina, 183
'burying the parcel', 83–4
Bush, Barbara, 72

'Cat's in the Cradle' (song, Chapin), 28
causes of regrets, 82–5, 176–7
change, accepting, 144
Chapin, Harry, 28
'child' role, 58
children
  concept of value of money, 111,
    115–19
  contact lost with parents, 41
  contact with their grandparents, 25
  effect of relationships, 131
  giving time and attention to, 27–9
  health, 150–51
  listening to, 92–3
  praising, 100, 137–40
  relationships with parents, 101–2,
    104–6
  self-blame, 14–15, 40–41, 104
  teaching resilience to, 9–13
  using social media, 34–6
claustrophobia, 78
commission, regrets of, 2
communication, 96–7, 172
  feelings, 88–91, 94–6, 159, 181
  improving skills, 98–9
  listening skills, 62, 91–3, 175
  in relationships, 141
  standing up for yourself, 93–6
comparisons with others, 165
compliments, 98
compromise in relationships, 101

conflict
  between friends, 57–8
  in relationships, 142–3
control
  giving children a feeling of, 10–11
  over past events, 6, 13–15, 40–42
convenience food, 152
cosmetic surgery, 159–60
counselling, 105, 191–202
  for relationship difficulties, 134, 145

death
  apologizing to someone after, 71
  mourning, 123–6, 178–9
decision-making, 172
descriptive praise, 138–9
detox diets, 161
Dickens, Charles, 106, 122
dinnertime game, 139–40
discouragement from achieving
    dreams, 82–5
divorce, 134
  of friends, 59–60
dreams
  achieving later in life, 76–80, 85–6
  discouragement, 82–5
  not achieving, 74–5

eating habits, 151–3, 157–8, 161
electronic media, 36–7, 52–3
envy, 6

failure, 3
  acceptance of, 12–13
  anticipation of, 12, 75
families
  discussing things over dinner, 139–40
  extended, 26–7
  health and fitness, 157–8
  mutual support, 102
  shared responsibilities, 31–2
  spending time together, 17–19,
    24–9, 30–33, 35, 36–7, 43

staying in touch, 172–3
  as support networks, 47
  value of money in, 111–13
feelings
  acknowledging, 143
  disguising, 123
  effect of cosmetic surgery, 159
  showing, 88–91, 94–6, 181
fitness, 150–51, 153–4, 156–7, 161
food, 151–3, 157–8, 161
forgiveness, 62, 70, 175
friends
  breaking off friendships, 54–5
  conflict with partners, 58–9
  divorce, 59–60
  keeping in touch with, 53–4, 61–2
  mixing groups, 60–61
  online, 33–4, 51–3
  problems with, 56–8, 102–3,
    105, 164
  as support networks, 46–51
  valued over family, 26–7

gossip, 56–7
grandparents, keeping contact with,
  25
gratitude, 163–4, 182
grieving, 123–6, 178–9

health, 150–58, 161–2
help
  asking for, 18
  professional, 84, 105, 134, 145,
    191–202
Herrick, Robert, 99
Hippocrates, 151
housework, shared, 31–2

'I' statements, 93–6
ideas-storming, 38–40, 172

Jefferson, Thomas, 153
jobs for teenagers, 118–19

Kennedy, John F., 153
kindness, 61, 166, 182
  to yourself, 184

Lawrence, D.H., 189
learning from regrets, 12, 70, 145–7,
    179–81
life phases, 17
life–work balance, 16–19, 28, 30–32, 54
listening skills, 62, 91–3, 175
loan companies, 115–16
long-term effects of past regrets, 4–5
love, expressing, 88–90, 181–3
lying, 144–5

marriage see relationships
memories, evoking, 26, 42
Miller, Arthur, 189
Milne, A.A., 153
mistakes
  admitting to, 67
  learning from, 12, 70, 145–7,
    179–81
Molière, 20
money, 110
  budgeting, 114–19, 120–22
  emotional value, 111–14
Montgomery, L.M., 85
mourning, 123–6, 178–9

'no', saying to friends, 55, 105
nostalgia, 6–7

older people, achievements, 76–7
omission, regrets of, 2–3
opinions of others, 132–4
opportunities
  missed, 6–7
  taken later in life, 78

'parent' role, 58
parents, 3–6, 8–9, 13–15, 100, 101–2,
    103–4, 106, 171

effect on future relationships,
    131–2
  keeping contact with, 25, 28–9
  lack of money, 110
  parenting skills, 172
  repeating patterns with own
    children, 15–16
  teaching children to budget, 115–19
  time lost with, 41
past
  control over, 6, 13–15, 40–42
  desire to change, 3–5
perspective, sense of, 145
phases
  of life, 17
  of a relationship, 142
phobias as barriers, 78, 79–80
piercings, 158–9
pocket money, 116–17
Pope, Alexander, 146
pornography, online, 36
positive thinking, 183, 184–5
poverty, 110
praise
  excessive, 100
  need for, 137–40
priorities, 173
  in friendships, 50, 54
  in life, 19, 30–32
problem solving, 11
professional help, 84, 105, 191–202
  for relationship difficulties, 134, 145

questions, open and closed, 10, 93

Random Acts of Kindness (RAKs), 182
reflective listening, 92–3
relationships, 99–102, 130–32, 177–8
  apologizing in, 68–70
  breaking up, 59–60, 134
  effects of past regrets, 4–5
  improving, 140–45
  maintaining, 135–7

other people's opinions, 132–4
praise in, 138–9
spending time together, 17–19,
    29, 35
'toxic', 54, 102–6, 164
remorse, 63–71, 175
resentment, 62
resilience
    effect of upbringing, 5–6, 8–9
    lack of, 8–9
    need for, 7–8
    teaching in children, 9–13
responsibilities, shared within the
        family, 31–2
responsibility, taking, 175
roles in friendships (child, parent,
        adult), 57–8
routine, 43

seize the day, 146–7
self
    apologizing to, 64–5
    making time for, 184
self-blame, 14–15, 40–41, 104
self-confidence, 132–4
self-criticism, 98–9
self-esteem, 12–13, 68, 154, 183–4
    body image, 162
Shusterman, Neal, 86
siblings, apologizing to, 67
sleep, 161
smoking, 155–6, 161
social media, 33–7, 51–2
    downside, 52–3
spontaneity, 99
    in relationships, 136

standing up for yourself, 93–6
strength of mind see resilience
support networks, 46–51
    online, 51–2

talents, nurturing, 163
tattoos, 158–9
teenagers
    listening to, 92–3
    money management, 117–19
thanks, expressing, 90–91, 182
Thoreau, Henry David, 170
time
    balancing, 16–19, 28, 24–32, 54
    wishing away, 166
'toxic' relationships, 54, 102–6, 164
travel, desire to, 81
treating yourself, 184
trust in others' ability, 10–11
Twain, Mark, 2

upbringing, 3–6, 8–9, 13–15, 100,
    101–2, 103–4, 106, 171
    effect on future relationships,
        131–2
    lack of money, 110
    learning to budget, 115–19
    repeating with own children,
        15–16

work–life balance, 16–19, 28, 30–32,
    54
working hours for teenagers, 118–19
worst-case scenarios, 12

'you' statements, 94, 95